Essays in Faith and Learning

Essays in Faith and Learning

A Festschrift in Honor of Dr. Song Nai Rhee

Edited by
MICK BOLLENBAUGH
and STEVEN GOETZ

Foreword by
JOSEPH D. WOMACK

☙PICKWICK *Publications* • Eugene, Oregon

ESSAYS IN FAITH AND LEARNING
A Festschrift in Honor of Dr. Song Nai Rhee

Copyright © 2015 Wipf and Stock Publishers. All rights reserved. Except for brief quotations in critical publications or reviews, no part of this book may be reproduced in any manner without prior written permission from the publisher. Write: Permissions, Wipf and Stock Publishers, 199 W. 8th Ave., Suite 3, Eugene, OR 97401.

Pickwick Publications
An Imprint of Wipf and Stock Publishers
199 W. 8th Ave., Suite 3
Eugene, OR 97401

www.wipfandstock.com

ISBN 13: 978-1-62564-225-7

Cataloguing-in-Publication data:

Essays in faith and learning : a festschrift in honor of Dr. Song Nai Rhee / edited by Mick Bollenbaugh and Steve Goetz ; foreword by Joseph D. Womack.

xviii + 138 p. ; 23 cm. Includes bibliographical references.

ISBN 13: 978-1-62564-225-7

1. Rhee, Song Nai. 2. Church and education. 3. Church and college. 4. Colleges and universities—Religion. 5. Christian universities and colleges—United States. 6. Church colleges—United States. I. Bollenbaugh, Mick. II. Goetz, Steve. III. Womack, Joseph D.

BV1464 E85 2015

Manufactured in the U.S.A.   12/04/2015

Unless otherwise noted, Scripture quotations come from the New Revised Standard Version Bible. Copyright © 1989, Division of Christian Education of the National Council of the Churches of Christ in the United States of America. Used by permission. All rights reserved.

Scripture quotations marked (NIV) are taken from the Holy Bible, New International Version®, NIV®. Copyright ©1973, 1978, 1984, 2011 by Biblica, Inc.™ Used by permission of Zondervan. All rights reserved worldwide. www.zondervan.com The "NIV" and "New International Version" are trademarks registered in the United States Patent and Trademark Office by Biblica, Inc.™

Scripture quotations marked (ESV) are from the ESV® Bible (The Holy Bible, English Standard Version®), copyright © 2001 by Crossway, a publishing ministry of Good News Publishers. Used by permission. All rights reserved.

Contents

Contributors | vii

Foreword | ix
—Joseph D. Womack

Introduction: A Festschrift in Honor of Dr. Song Nai Rhee | xiii
—Steven Goetz

Abbreviations | xviii

1 Christian *Paideia* and the Educational Vision of Song Nai Rhee | 1
—Mick Bollenbaugh and Steve Goetz

2 Spirituality, Ancient Traditions, and the Modern Workplace | 25
—Michael Kennedy

3 Biblical Preaching and Rhetorical Criticism | 43
—George Knox

4 The Scribe Who Has Been Trained for the Kingdom: A Biblical Theological Perspective on Faith and Learning | 64
—Dennis R. Lindsay

5 The Transformational Power of Faculty Mentorship: Engaging Newly Enrolled Students toward Academic and Life Success | 80
—Angela Long

6 Sixty Years of Change and Challenge in Christian Higher Education: During the Times of Song Nai Rhee | 93
—Gerald (Gary) Tiffin

7 The New Creation Motif in the Hebrew Bible | 108
—Yung Y. Yang

8 Faith and Learning—Thoughts from a Former Academic Dean | 128
—Song Nai Rhee

Song Nai Rhee

Mick Bollenbaugh

Steven Goetz

Contributors

Mick Bollenbaugh is Professor of Philosophy and Biblical Studies at Northwest Christian University. Mick has authored numerous publications and writings, including *Redemption and Responsibility: A Few Hours with George Alder* (co-edited with Gary Tiffin) (1999), "The Place of Reason of the Stone-Campbell Movement," and "Eugene Sanderson," both of the *Stone-Campbell Encyclopedia* (2005).

Steven Goetz is Professor of History and Philosophy at Northwest Christian University. His primary teaching schedule includes courses in the humanities, history, philosophy, and religion. He brings over 25 years of teaching experience to the classroom. Steven is active in scholarship and has presented numerous papers on religious, historical, and philosophical subjects to various scholarly societies.

Song Nai Rhee is Academic Dean Emeritus at Northwest Christian University. He is author of numerous scholarly articles and books in the areas of biblical studies, archaeology, and anthropology.

Michael Kennedy is emeritus Faculty Professor in Business and Management at Northwest Christian University. He hold the M.Div. from Yale and DBA from Nova Southeastern University.

George M. Knox is Professor Emeritus of New Testament and Homiletics at Northwest Christian University in Eugene, Oregon. He is also an ordained minister and served Christian churches in Oregon for nearly forty years.

Dennis Lindsay is Vice President for Academic Affairs & Dean of Faculty at Northwest Christian University. He is the author of *Josephus and Faith* (1993) and *Believing in Jesus: Studies in the Gospel of John* (2006).

Contributors

Angela Long serves as a researcher, educator, and consultant on retention issues in higher education. She is co-editor of a national book series titled "Innovative Ideas for Community Colleges" and recently published her first book: *America's Forgotten Student Population*. Angela has shared her findings across the nation. She holds an EdD in Leadership from OSU and is a graduate of NCU, earning the MA in School Counseling and BA in Elementary Education.

Gerald (Gary) Tiffin succeeded Song Nai Rhee as NCC Provost in 1998. Since 2006 he has taught in and directed the EdD program at George Fox University. He was Dean (16 years) and taught (26 years) at Hope International University after teaching at William Jessup University (then San Jose Bible College) for seven years. He holds a PhD from Stanford University in history of education.

Andy Yang is emeritus Professor of Economics at California State University, Sacramento (PhD in economics, University of Oregon, 1974), and has received a MPhil (theology) from Northwest Christian University in December 2014.

Foreword

Joseph D. Womack

IN THE SPRING OF 1987 I sat at one end of a long rectangular desk in the office of the Vice President for Academic Affairs at Northwest Christian College opposite a man to whom I had only previously been introduced. I wasn't there by choice but by the direction of my father, James Womack, who recently had been named as NCC's president. Following an unsuccessful attempt at collegiate success at another institution, I was there to discuss my future. Although I couldn't have known it at the time, it was a future that would be, in many ways, influenced profoundly by the teaching, encouragement, and story of the man sitting opposite me that morning, Dr. Song Nai Rhee.

Among the many things I have gained from my relationship with Dr. Rhee (aside from the blessing of meeting his daughter, Ruby to whom I have been married for over 20 years), perhaps the most compelling was an appreciation for a commitment to learning informed and motivated by a sincere Christian faith. As a student at NCC, now Northwest Christian University (NCU) I came to know Dr. Song Nai Rhee as an excellent teacher possessing deep wisdom and a superior intellect. As his son-in-law I have come to know him as a compassionate and dedicated family man. As NCU's tenth president, I have come to understand that he is not only our institution's most accomplished academic, he is perhaps the most compelling story in our 120 years as an institution of higher education.

Song Nai Rhee was born in September of 1935 into a prominent family history of over 600 years of Confucian faith. The innocence of his youth was attacked along with his village during the invasion of South Korea by

Foreword

the Communist North Koreans in June of 1950. His family lost everything. Although they were saved by the American military who intervened on behalf of South Korea, they were now desperately poor and in constant danger. They endured three years of night raids by guerilla fighters burning villages and taking and torturing captives.

After Song's school was burned to the ground he sought work with the American military hoping to improve his English—working in the laundry and eventually as an interpreter in combat zones. He was later able to return to his schooling through the support of an American helicopter pilot, attending a Christian institution where he eventually accepted Jesus Christ as Lord. Following his graduation he obtained a list of Christian colleges in the U.S. from the American Consulate in Seoul and wrote to each concerning his hopes. He received one reply. Ross Griffith, president of Northwest Christian University, responded to his letter offering a full-tuition scholarship and the promise to assist in further expenses should he be able to find his way to the States.

After having saved just enough for a plane ticket from Seoul to Portland, Oregon, and a bus ticket to Eugene, Song arrived at the doorstep of Dr. Griffith (NCU president 1944–1965) in the winter of 1955. He had with him only $4 and a small duffle containing a change of clothes and Bible. The subsequent years would see him through graduating with a bachelor's degree in 1958 while receiving NCU's highest student honor, the Kendall E. Burke Award. Song would further his studies at Butler University in Indianapolis, Indiana, where he received an additional bachelor's degree and a Master's of Arts. He then completed a PhD in Hebrew & Biblical Studies from Dropsie University in Philadelphia.

Following the completion of his doctoral studies Song was called to serve on the NCU faculty for Biblical Studies in 1963, eventually ascending to the role of Academic Dean and Vice President in 1984. In that role he oversaw a significant expansion of course offerings and majors. During a long academic career he obtained a second PhD in archaeology from the University of Oregon and published numerous scholarly articles and books. He excelled in the classroom and led archaeological excavations in Israel and Korea. Retiring in 2000 after 37 years of service he is remember by hundreds of graduates as well as former faculty and colleagues as a favored mentor, deeply committed to excellence through the integration of scholarly study and faith.

Foreword

The notion of the integration of faith and learning that defined so much of Song's academic endeavors has always existed at the core of NCU's mission. Almost exactly 120 years ago Eugene Sanderson founded a college with a profound notion for education that endures today. In an advertisement that ran on October 15, 1895, in the local paper Sanderson described his intention for the NCU experience, "It is desired that our students shall acquire proficiency, at once scholarly and practical, for immediate service in all departments of Christian work."

Evident at its very beginning is a powerful core objective for this institution that has long endured—the integration of the intellect with Christian faith and service. This integration, the simultaneous existence of the two goals of academic rigor and faith-inspired practical service, has served the institution well finding semantic variation through time. It is here, at the point of integration, where we realize the value of intellectual inquiry through the lens of the Christian worldview. This is where we discover that true learning is realized best through practice, and that it must both enlighten the mind and improve the human condition. And it is here, at NCU, where Song committed his work as a student, professor and administrator.

Due, in large part to Song Nai Rhee's impact, we continue to believe that the NCU experience builds on this rich tradition, one that seeks to open students' minds to the vast expanse of human expression and thought: We continue to promote a greater understanding of our world; to enable students to seek and discern what is good and true; and to build on and find new expressions to inspire within students the desire to seek solutions to the challenges we face in society and opportunities for service in our world. Song Nai Rhee has been and continues to be a major contributor to the ongoing status of these educational values at NCU.

Currently we face the challenge and opportunity to think of what NCU can be at its very best. We have come to use words to describe NCU like wisdom, faith, and service. These are meant to communicate to the public our ethos, to promote and market who we are, but more importantly to remind us of our long held commitments as a learning community. Wisdom we perceive to be the progression beyond knowledge, combining what we know, believe, and do. Knowledge that finds expression and reason within a commitment to our faith in Jesus opens our hearts and minds to the very wisdom of God—as the apostle Paul reminded us in his charge to consider our calling in First Corinthians: "It is because of him that you are in Christ

Foreword

Jesus, who has become for us wisdom from God—that is our righteousness, holiness, and redemption" (1 Cor 1:30, NIV).

At NCU faith is still central to all we do—to know and make known our Lord and Savior. Our efforts within and without the classroom center around an effort to think and act Christianly—to consider our relationship with God as central to our pursuit of calling. And our calling points to a life of service to the church, our communities, and to one another. Built upon a foundation for higher education constructed by those who served before us, we remain convinced that the transformational experience of the pursuit of *wisdom* centered on *faith* will find expression in acts of *service*.

As we find new opportunities for the mission of Northwest Christian University it is imperative that we honor and recognize the foundations upon which that mission is erected, including those individuals who learned, taught, and embodied those values. Such is the purpose of the Festschrift written and compiled in honor of Song. The idea of two long-serving and distinguished professors, Drs. Steve Goetz and Mick Bollenbaugh, this work examines the thoughts of current and retired NCU faculty, administration, and staff as well as a recent graduate of our Masters of Theology program. In the following chapters you will find an excellent compilation of thinking regarding the integration of faith and learning from numerous perspectives. It is my hope and prayer that you will be blessed upon this reading and encouraged, as I have been, by the example of Dr. Song Nai Rhee.

Introduction

A Festschrift in Honor of Dr. Song Nai Rhee

Steven Goetz

THE EDITORS ARE HONORED to present this Festschrift as an occasion of celebration for the profound contribution that Dr. Song Nai Rhee has made to Northwest Christian University through his many years of service. Though to date his individual achievements are notable and numerous, some of his most important contributions are those that have been wrought by impacts he brought to bear on colleagues, students and the scholarly world at large. For this reason, the editors solicited and collected articles and essays from those who have been inspired by him in their ongoing careers, research and writing. The unifying theme of "integration of faith and learning" (an idea central to the concerns of Dr. Rhee) has been chosen to bring coherence to the various contributions gathered here.

The idea for this Festschrift arose on the bittersweet occasion of the "celebration of life" that was held in NCU's the MEC for Mr. Skip Stock (a dear friend of Dr. Rhee and NWCU) who had passed away in October of 2012 at the untimely age of 67. The editors of this work were struck by the way that the gathering to remember and celebrate Skip's life had the power to resurrect its exemplary courage and power in all who had been touched by it. And it seemed that everywhere Skip's achievements were mentioned, NCU's and, particularly Song Nai Rhee's, presence was there too in companionship. What a great idea, we thought, to parlay this spirit into the future by celebrating Dr. Rhee's achievements in his own lifetime and, so, the notion of this Festschrift was conceived by the editors.

Introduction

We were fortunate that a publishing venture called Wipf and Stock Publishers, Inc. had been pioneered in Eugene, Oregon in the 90s by John Wipf of Archives Bookshop in Pasadena and Jon Stock of Windows Booksellers in Eugene to combat the troubling rate at which academic books were going out of print due to prohibitive increases in publishing costs and loss of awareness and interest. Because of the family's connection (Skip Stock was Jon Stock's brother) and because of the commonality of vision, Wipf and Stock Publishers, Inc. were approached with the idea of the Festschrift for Dr. Rhee and were immediately encouraging and enthusiastic. Now, nearly three years later, the Festschrift has finally come to fruition and the editors hope and pray that it will be as helpful for the promotion of Christian faith and the integration of faith and learning as is the life of Skip Stock, the work of Wipf and Stock Publishers and the complementary visions of Dr. Song Nai Rhee, especially in his exemplary work at NCC for the promotion of the integration of faith and learning in Christian higher education.

A brief introduction to Dr. Song Nai Rhee, particularly in connection to NCU, is in order here, however, not in the riveting prose and detail that you will find in chapter 8 of this work, "Faith and Learning: Thoughts From a Former Academic Dean." Rhee was born in South Korea in 1935 and was only 15 years of age when the Korean War broke out. The friendship of an American GI, led to the funding of Rhee's education in Korea at a Christian School and soon to his dramatic conversion to faith in Jesus Christ. In the winter of 1955/56, again through the influence and assistance of the American GI, Rhee arrived on American soil, in Eugene, Oregon, where he immediately began studying at Northwest Christian College (a Christian liberal arts institution that had been founded in 1895 right next door to the University of Oregon).

Through hard work and determination, he rapidly overcame the challenges of being a recent immigrant to America, completing his B.Th. degree at NCC in 1958. In the ensuing 5 years, Rhee completed additional undergraduate and graduate (rather than repeating undergraduate) degrees in history, political science, ancient Hebrew language and literature and finally the Ph.D. degree in Old Testament Studies from Dropsie University in 1963. (Rhee earned a second doctoral degree from the University of Oregon in Archaeology and Anthropology in 1984).

Dr. Rhee began his long teaching career at NCC in the same year that he received his first doctoral degree. He quickly became a beloved

Introduction

and respected presence on the campus that became the foundation for his influence and importance for the school, not only for his academic knowledge but for his passion for Christ and his theological wisdom. His premier course in these years was "Eighth Century Prophets," a must-take course at the time. It was a transformative experience for the many students who remember it fondly to this day. Rhee was known for teaching the Old Testament with faithful reverence but also with historical fidelity to context, a product of the historiographical discipline he had learned from his advanced historical studies. Of course, as students were challenged to think more deeply about the Biblical texts, occasional controversies were stirred up in his classes. However, students were encouraged to incorporate new insights into an expanding awareness of God's relation with his creation and his creatures. This twenty-year period of Rhee's career at NCC marked the true beginning of what would develop into his unique, nuanced understanding of integration of faith and learning. (Cf. Chapter 1 of this volume, Bollenbaugh and Goetz, "Christian *Paideia* and the Educational Vision of Dr. Song Nai Rhee).

The second phase of Song Nai Rhee's career, beginning in 1984 with his appointment as Dean and then Provost of the College, was dominated by administrative. For NCC, as for many other small Christian Colleges, these decades were occupied with broadening the curriculum and focus of Christian higher education from a focus on ministry to a full range of majors and career training choices (Cf. Chapter 6 of this work Tiffin, "Sixty Years of Change and Challenge in Christian Higher Education: during the Times of Song Nai Rhee"). The urgencies of this period for NCC were magnified in that the school was in serious financial jeopardy and, consequently, at risk of having its academic accreditation suspended and possibly even withdrawn by the Northwest Commission on Colleges and Universities. Without going into all the details of how this was brought about, it is today generally acknowledged that with Dr. Song Nai Rhee as Dean of Academic Affairs and James Womack as President, NCC was able to remodel its curriculum and institutional way to "save the College" financially without losing its soul as a Christian institution of higher education, virtually a case of steering the school successfully between a perilous rock and a hard place of its history. Rhee's commitment to the Christian Church/Disciples of Christ heritage of "books and the BOOK" and constant fixation on his unique vision of the integration of faith and learning were vital to his (and Womack's) success. When in 1995 a campus renovation project linking the

Introduction

chapel building with the Kellenberger library building was completed and then dedicated, Dr Rhee spoke these important words:

> At Northwest Christian College, students are expected to acquire knowledge of nature, philosophy, art, literature, history, government, and many other academic disciplines as part of their total education, as are students at the University of Oregon next door. However, here at NCC we expect our students to go beyond the knowledge of nature, philosophy, art, literature, history, and government and know, in their search for a free and meaningful life, God who, we believe, is the source of all knowledge, all truths, and all that is good, beautiful and noble, and is truly worthy of our worship and our praise.
>
> That is the distinctive mission of Northwest Christian College. Therefore, it is so fitting not only symbolically, but also practically, that the library and the chapel have been joined together. When we enter this beautifully renovated building, we come into a building that houses tens of thousands of books and other learning resources as well as a place of prayer and worship. Under one roof, we shall move back and forth, from the place of learning to the place of prayer, from learning to faith and from faith to learning, as we seek to enrich our own lives and those of others whom we serve.
>
> The joining of the College's library with the chapel therefore offers a very special meaning to us all. It serves as a powerful symbol, speaking loudly about NCC's mission, purpose, and goal: faith, learning, and service.[1]

Dr Rhee retired from NCC in 2000, following a fifty-four-year career of service to the school. He continues to reside in Eugene with his wife Sue, herself a retired distinguished director of the Kellenberger Library. Dr. Rhee holds the title of Professor Emeritus at what is now NCU and continues to be an active and influential presence on the campus. He also remains active in the Eugene and Lane County community through his op/ed pieces on Asian politics, economics, and trade, which regularly appear in the Eugene *Register-Guard*. (For a sample, see his most recent piece on the Japanese Government of Abe Shinzo.[2]) Dr Rhee is an active visiting scholar at the University of Oregon in the Center for Asian and Pacific

---

1. Dr. Song Nai Rhee, Academic Dean Message delivered at dedication of Chapel/Library renovation, September 13, 1995.

2. http://registerguard.com/rg/opinion/33009722-78/abe-must-stop-whitewashing.html.csp.

Introduction

Studies of the University where he pursues research in Ancient Korea and it's demographic, cultural, and technological contributions to early Japan. Since his retirement he has published several important articles in the prestigious peer journal *Asian Perspectives*. Ever the one for embracing new projects (and surprising us all with new talents), he has recently published a work of historical fiction centered upon the life of Nashimoto Masako, the Japanese princess who was married off to a Korean prince, titled *Beautiful as a Rainbow: Nashimoto Masako, a Japanese Princess against All Odds for Love, Life, and Happiness*. The work continues to attract a growing fan base and, who knows what else is next.

Such a life of accomplishment and service demands recognition and so the editors and the contributors of this work have joined together to produce a work that we hope will be a fitting tribute to the focus of our attention. May the readers of the essays of this Festschrift be as challenged and inspired in reading them as the contributors themselves were inspired to write them through the incomparable example of Dr. Song Nai Rhee.

Abbreviations

CLAU	Christian liberal arts university
NCC	Northwest Christian College
NCU	Northwest Christian University

TDNT   *Theological Dictionary of the New Testament*, edited by Gerhard Kittel and Gerhard Friedrich. Translated by Geoffrey W. Bromiley. Grand Rapids: Eerdmans, 1969–

1

Christian *Paideia* and the Educational Vision of Song Nai Rhee

Mick Bollenbaugh and Steve Goetz

"I fear the man of a single book"

—Thomas Aquinas

WITHOUT EXAGGERATION, IT IS appropriate to say that Dr. Song Nai Rhee is a central figure in the history and culture of Northwest Christian College/Northwest Christian University (since 2008). Many students who attended NCC/NCU during his long years of service as teacher and administrator would unhesitatingly name him as the most important and impactful teacher of their NCC experience. Likewise, his fellow NCC/NCU colleagues and many other researchers working in the fields of Old Testament studies, archaeology and history would cite him as the school's most distinguished academic due to his meticulous scholarship and exemplary professional practice. Those who have had the privilege of knowing him more personally (the authors have a combined acquaintance of 56 years with Rhee), appreciate him as a superlative Christian teacher-scholar and as an indefatigable advocate of Christian higher education. Under these considerations, we think it is fitting to write this essay in honor of his many contributions to the NCC/NCU community and, more particularly, to focus on an important idea close to his heart, viz. the integration of faith and learning, both how he understands this concept and also how it has been complemented by other distinguished thinkers who have wrestled with the idea in recent times.

Rhee's views on the integration of faith and learning can be gleaned from a speech he made at the inauguration of Dr. Joseph Womack as the tenth president of Northwest Christian University on October 7, 2010. His speech was based upon a motto inscribed on a plaque on the wall of the NCC library, placed there in 1957 when Rhee was himself just a student of about one year. The motto reads: "The books and the Book. That we may know Him." Taken as a whole, the motto directs attention to three distinct things, learning (science, reason), faith (the Bible) and the person of Jesus Christ (that we may know Him). The first two things for education in the context of Christian higher education (books and the Book) are mentioned as important and placed almost upon an equally important level (although only one of them is capitalized). The importance of the third thing (that we may know Him) is elevated as the primary end for the other two, viz., a personal and life transforming relationship with the living Christ. In these few words, Rhee sees the purpose of his own life's work as well as a path for how faith and learning may be integrated (Cf. Chap. 8 "Faith and Learning—Thoughts from a Former Academic Dean" where Rhee shares the compelling story of his pilgrimage from Confucianism to Christian faith, his journey to America, and genesis of his philosophy of Christian education).

From Rhee's mindful connection of the "books and the Book," spring a variety of themes central to any robust and fully developed Christian philosophy of education. The mutuality and relationality of faith and learning is basic to his thinking about how learning should occur in the Christian liberal arts university (henceforth abbreviated as CLAU). This work is driven by a felt need to repair any rift that may exist between faith and learning in many educational institutions that are religious in nature. For Rhee, Christian academics who appreciate and understand the importance of faith and learning integration are called to read and study critically, thoughtfully, cautiously, and faithfully, guided by the conviction that the discovery of truth in all its forms is a divine and normative process. Such a pursuit of truth is concerned to recover a credible Christian witness in a

Christian *Paideia* and the Educational Vision of Song Nai Rhee

world that hardly seems to know what to do with itself on matters of education. Without the guiding principle of "the books and the Book" underpinning the curriculum of the CLAU, functioning as the locus of worship and praise directed toward God, education becomes an unfortunate stranger to that which is thought to truly integrate faith and learning. As a remedy to this problem, Rhee's thinking brings academics, disciplined by theology, front and center into the culture of the CLAU.

Such an aspiration as Rhee's gives heartfelt expression of the deepest hopes of the CLAU's desire to persuade Christian students that they can have their vocational aspirations come to fruition in an educational environment supportive of their faith convictions. In the context of the CLAU, instruction in the liberal arts is modified by the integration of faith and learning in such a way that Christian students expect their faith to be nurtured and challenged while also being excellently prepared to compete for careers in a largely secular job market. By making an appeal to "the books and the Book," Rhee offers a philosophy of education that potentially unifies the disciplines, driven by the notion that all truth is God's truth seen ultimately in an intimate knowledge of Jesus Christ ("that we may know Him").

As a point of distinction, the CLAU does not intentionally pit itself against institutions that are self-described as Bible Colleges nor those known as secular universities. Rather, the CLAU finds its *raison d'etre* on its own unique ground when it calls for a unity of the disciplines along theological lines. Such a unity is held together by theology in a way that distinguishes itself from the fragmented curriculums of the secular university (as will be discussed later in the work of Alasdair McIntyre) and the way such disciplines are often missing from the curriculums of Bible Colleges.

In a historically ironic development those who might oppose the integration of faith and learning on intellectual grounds (secular universities) are allies with those from the camp of faith who fear that learning carries with it a set of dynamics whose very nature undermines the concerns of faith. If learning is seen as an assailant against the citadel of faith then a peace accord that brings faith and learning together is not only undesirable but flatly dangerous for matters of religious belief. Hence, the seemingly separate categories of faith and learning might have mutual suspicions of one another.

From the learning side of academe there are legitimate worries that those from the arena of faith will fail to maintain standards of intellectual rigor and honesty. Such worries are that faith-based institutions will be interested in defending certain prescribed doctrines or theological claims by a tacit move that insulates these claims from rational critique. The said doctrines are made "holy" so as to immunize them in a way that protects against any arguments that may reveal flaws in a doctrine thought to be key to the faith tradition in question. A faith-based institution must be vigilant in its efforts to hold to the highest standards of intellectual pursuit and its natural corollary, academic freedom. To make their voices heard faith-based colleges and universities must not shy away from inquiry that potentially poses a threat to its doctrinal positions. To do so only serves to heighten suspicions that faith-based institutions are not serious about learning or scholarship in its most robust sense. Rhee himself addresses this concern by vigorously rejecting the notion that integration of faith and learning is equivalent to apologetics. In his words:

> Integration of faith and learning is NOT reconciliation of knowledge and faith. It is not an exercise of Christian apologetic. That is, it is not an effort to reconcile math, history, or chemistry with the Christian faith or vice versa. **Such efforts are impractical and impossible** [text emboldened by Rhee]. Rather, integration of faith and learning is an effort to bring Christian meaning into all knowledge in light of the transcendent Christian faith and worldview. It is a conscious effort to help students become informed of the message of the Christian gospel and the fundamental Christian values and to become impacted by them in their life and work.

On the other side of the coin, those who advocate for an educational practice informed by faith are justified in criticizing educators in the secular world who complain about the inconsistencies between faith and learning while being driven by certain agendas, even vendettas, of their own. Given the social climate in America and that of the world at large, Christian educators have good reason to be concerned to resist versions of learning that are shorn of faith and meaningful reference to God. They are rightly determined to seek to establish pedagogical systems that lay a foundation for character and provide a sense of focus and purpose for life, albeit without violating canons of academic discipline and creditable scholarship. And there is a long history of a partnership existing between values and learning that is modeled in Greek natural theology and calls to a consideration of being open to that which is higher.[1] Presumably, most if not all educational

---

1. Taylor, *A Secular Age*, 288, 613.

institutions seek to link their educational systems with a set of core values that will conclude with their embodiment in their student's lives. Rhee's concern is to get all Christian educational institutions and all Christian educators to see that in our study of "the books" and in our concentration upon the canons of faith through our study of "the Book" that we not forget that the ultimate purpose of it all is "that we might know Him."

Hence, in Rhee's understanding, the CLAU steers a middle course between the respective educational visions of the Bible College and the secular university. In the first instance, Bible Colleges are usually oriented toward training students to do work in individual congregational settings. Whether this work is as pastor, youth pastor, music minister, missionary, or children's ministries, the educational niche of the Bible College is to train people for vocation in the context of congregational life. Its seeming polar opposite is the secular university that focuses on educating students in a variety of recognized academic disciplines, preparing such students for careers that are not by nature religious. Rhee's concept of the CLAU offers a curriculum not unlike what is found in the secular university but is distinguished from the secular university by giving these disciplines a theological orientation and a spiritual practice.

Rhee's thinking about and commitment to the integration of faith and learning forms a natural bridge to an educational concept deeply embedded in ancient Greek life and thought, viz. that which is often called *paideia*. *Paideia* carries considerable freight when it is seen that nearly all cultures educate and discipline their citizens by helping them absorb a set of virtues necessary for the proper function of the polis. Hence, a rough and ready definition of *paideia* carries the various meanings of education, discipline, spiritual culture, and development of character.[2]

Key to this essay is to show the way in which the essential notion of "the books and the Book, that we may know Him" reflects what we might call Christian *paideia*. The educational power of *paideia* in all its human settings transforms the lives of those who are exposed to its tenets and this is true for Christian culture as well. A culture that is appropriately called Christian will by its very nature have a *paideia* of its own that bears the weight of Christian values and learning. Because human beings usually strive to live in relationship with one another a cultural identity automatically ensues. Such an identity manifests itself in the way in which cultures work to transmit and immortalize their values in the lives of those who

---

2. Bertram, "*Paideia*," 5:596–97.

are part of its fabric. In Rhee's pattern of thinking, creating *paideia* is a universal human activity. Hence, it is expected that Christianity will form a *paideia* that educates and disciplines its members according to the values of the gospel of Jesus Christ.

Paideia as Culture and Education

The following discussion is intended as an enhancement to Rhee's thinking regarding the integration of faith and learning. The approach we take in this section is a modest one meant to support what Rhee offers as an educational vision of faith and learning integration. Part of our goal is to offer a provisional and developing contribution to a promising avenue of conversation that seeks to bring "the books and the Book" together in a pedagogical vision that upholds the value of the integration of faith and learning. We proceed from the assertion that the vision of integration is incomplete and futile without the assumption of the goal of Christian higher education being the knowledge of Jesus Christ. Our approach begins by giving attention to three contemporary individuals (Werner Jaeger, Alasdair McIntyre, and Stanley Hauerwas) whose ideas are suitable for advancing the project of gaining clarity about the unique educational vision of the CLAU. The thoughts of these three academics demonstrate an interesting and compelling parallel to Rhee's sentiments on matters of faith and learning integration.

Werner Jaeger, Alasdair McIntyre, and Stanley Hauerwas have added clarity to the larger conversation about the integration of faith and learning in the CLAU, though they have done so without specific intent. That is to say, these individuals do not use the language of faith and learning integration per se. However, their historical, theological, and philosophical insights bring to bear a way of thinking about the integration of faith and learning in post-secondary institutions that are self-described as Christian. They give remarkable substance to the integration of faith and learning in a spirit that is strikingly parallel to what we have found in the thinking of Rhee. First, a cursory examination of the concept of *paideia* as set forth in the work of Jaeger in its classical context will be assessed. Second, a reflective synthesis of some contemporary thinking offered by McIntyre and Hauerwas about pedagogical issues as seen in the secular university will be explored as a presenting problem for the CLAU. We will tap into some relevant arguments found in these individuals in order to see how they might offer something fresh to the ongoing dialogue we have highlighted here in the thought of Rhee.

We believe that a synthesis of their reflections will create some of the needed substance that gets beyond the sometimes cloudy language that short-circuits an intelligible account of faith and learning integration. This is so because the high sounding words of the integration of faith and learning is often more style than substance in many of its contemporary iterations. Such words are bandied about as if we have a clear sense of what the integration of faith and learning means with precision. Part of our goal is to approach such conversations with care so as to keep the overall discussion at the organic level, i.e. a discussion always open to new and fresh language that leads to a volume of high quality thinking about this topic. Hence, we will draw on a few of the insights from the thinkers noted above as a means to add to the growing discussion of what it means to integrate faith and learning. We do so because left on its own the language of the integration of faith and learning creates a tangled web of problems, a proverbial Gordian knot that needs a vigilant and persistent effort on the part of Christian educators in order to gain some clarity about matters related to the integration of faith and learning.

Jaeger and the Roots of Early Christian Paideia

Rhee's thinking about and commitment to the integration of faith and learning forms a natural bridge to the definitions of *paideia* offered above. When fully orbed, the language of the "books and the Book that we may know him" is an expression of Christian culture and education, or paideia. A culture that is appropriately called Christian will by its very nature have a *paideia* of its own that bears the weight of Christian values and learning. The primary locus of such a culture is potentially found in the family of post-secondary institutions commonly known as CLAUs.

Werner Jaeger contributes to this conversation via his analysis of a distinctly Christian *paideia*. He sketches its historical and theological development wherein the early Christian *kerygma* penetrated the world around it.[3] Jaeger's understanding of the *paideia* that arose in Greek culture is a useful means to gain a clearer vision of what it means to speak of the "books and the Book" in the same breath and how such a sentiment participates in a vision of the integration of faith and learning. Hence, esteem

3 Jaeger, *Early Christianity and Greek Paideia*, 4–5.

for the Greek classics is a very promising and appropriate place to begin in a cogent construction of the integration of faith learning. Christian *paideia* is derivative and in some sense beholding to the views held by the Classical Greeks and the manner in which they educated their young. Jaeger's excellent work on paideia generally and Christian *paideia* specifically provides a superstructure for an ongoing discussion of how to think about the books and the book.

Jaeger helps us see the means by which Christianity generated its own unique *paideia* but did not become exclusivist or tribalist since it unapologetically employs the Greek language and makes its own activity a recitation of thought and ways of thinking found, for example, in rhetoric.[4] By doing so Christianity becomes a world religion and overcomes it exclusiveness. Consistency with a tradition that underpins Christianity's practice of non-exclusivity means that the ways in which education is delivered must give due consideration to the academic disciplines known as the liberal arts. Non-exclusivity does not mean that Christianity is a mere un-reflective hybrid of the Hellenistic world in which it was steeped. On the contrary, Christianity makes its own unique claims in polemical fashion but is cognizant of the contributions that the surrounding culture makes to the ways these claims are fashioned. In his analysis of *paideia*, Jaeger highlights the work of such central philosophical traditions as Platonism and thinkers like Philo, Clement, Origen, the Cappadocians, and Augustine.

The earliest Christian *paideia* was a composite of the dialectical interaction with the framework of the Hellenistic world and the unique features of the Christian *kerygma*. Most of the Church fathers and mothers would have been confused by any effort to cleave the Christian *kerygma* from Hellenism. Our theological forbearers implicitly understood that separating *kerygma* from Hellenism would de-nature the fabric of Christian *paideia*. Following the lines of this model, faith and learning then are co-belligerents in the project of generating a Christian *paideia*. Neither aspect exhibits a slavish dependence on the other, but instead is a thoughtful borrowing and synthesis of ideas. A full consideration of *paideia* in its Greek cultural setting is a means to present the Christian faith with the intellectual machinery it needed to find its place in the early centuries of its development. It may even be historically arguable as to whether Christianity could have been successful without the vehicle provided by the Greek classical tradition.

---

4. Ibid., 6

Christian *Paideia* and the Educational Vision of Song Nai Rhee

By way of example from Jaeger, Philo serves as a medium of Greek thought in the practice of natural theology.[5] Though natural theology is often repudiated by many of the Protestant reformers because of its reliance on a depraved human Reason, in such salient figures as Augustine, Anselm, and Aquinas, natural theology flourished because of its intentional connection to the ancient classical tradition. In Christian *paideia* then, there is a basic recognition that purism of learning or faith is neither possible nor desired. As Jaeger notes, the historical tradition from Origen to Basil, to Gregory of Nazianzus, and Gregory of Nyssa is very important in setting a template for discussions of faith and learning.[6] Assuming Jaeger's interpretation is correct, faith and learning are found to be in symbiosis and this symbiotic relationship is what produces Christian *paideia*. This cross fertilization of faith and learning observed in the kind of education cherished by the early Christian apologists is a model for what is ideally exhibited in the CLAU.

The conversation about *paideia*, then, is in many ways as old as, and really antedates, the Christian tradition itself. The conceptual role of *paideia* in the ancient Christian fathers and mothers ensured that no tension or hostility to the connection of faith and learning ever existed. For them such a tension is unthinkable. Unlike the modern educational context, there is no need to repair a relationship between faith and learning that has soured through an unfortunate set of historical circumstances. Rather, a *paideia* that draws on the best resources and insights of the Hellenistic world is an excellent example of a more natural relationship between faith and learning.

Faith and Learning:
Returning the Soul to God That We May Know Christ

According to Jaeger, Christian *paideia* is saved by the practices of philosophical theology.[7] Paideia, then, concerns itself with trying to create a unified culture. Early Christian thinkers such as Clement and Origen make definitive steps "toward the goal of a Christian civilization. . ."[8] Origen's work played a strong model for a kind of mutual adaptation between Greek culture and the Christian church to both the books and the book because

5. Ibid., 30–31.
6. Ibid., 50–51.
7. Ibid., 61
8. Ibid., 62.

Origen saw the common features shared by both Christianity and the Greek intellectual heritage.[9] Yet Christianity could still be an *altera civitas* in its attempt to live out the ideals of its *paideia*.

For example, a bridge between *paideia* and *kerygma* reveals the way in which the Church proclaims its message along the lines of the rhetorical models found in the Hellenic world. For Jaeger, this approach puts rhetoric and philosophy in the service of the Church.[10] In effect, there is a careful filtering and re-working of content found in Greek *paideia* and a tacit praise of a framework for Christian *paideia*.[11] This move reflects the assumption that such a framework is necessary for the spread of culture and its educational ideals. If Jaeger is right, a Christian *paideia* meets the demands for the development of the human person[12] and aspires to a form of education that represents an intentional nurturing of the soul. Origen then interprets Christianity and its historical mission in Greek philosophical terms.[13] As Jaeger notes, early Greek education traces its heritage from a Homeric mold that ultimately become synonymous with literature.[14] It is later that such a *paideia* becomes differentiated into what is referred to as the liberal arts that ultimately embraced rhetoric and philosophy. The arts "were related as pro-*paideia*, and philosophy, as Plato conceived it, became identical with *paideia* itself on its highest level."[15]

The Christian conception of *paideia*, as Gregory thought, corresponds to the Greek schematic[16] which included Classical Greek literature and rhetoric.[17] Similarly, Origen instructed his students to read the Greek philosophers because just as *paideia* consisted of the entire corpus of Greek literature, Christian *paideia* is found in the Bible."[18] The importance of this fact cannot be overstated since it indicates that while the Bible becomes the basis of Christian *paideia*, the literature of the Greeks is not then abandoned but still plays an important role yet in what is described in modern

9. Ibid.
10. Ibid., 78.
11. Ibid., 81–83.
12. Ibid., 86
13. Ibid., 68.
14. Ibid., 91.
15. Ibid.
16. Ibid.
17. Ibid., 92
18. Ibid.

Christian *Paideia* and the Educational Vision of Song Nai Rhee

parlance as the liberal arts. While the Bible has the position of authority in the educational growth of the Christian who is to be *imitatio Christi,* classical Greek literature is still highly valued as a part of moral formation. Such concern now becomes for the Christian the metamorphosis Paul speaks of in Romans 12.[19] For example, Gregory completes his analogy between Greek philosophical education and Christian theology via an investigation of Plato's *Laws*.[20] Hence, Christian *paideia* springs from its interaction with Greek educational ideals. Greek philosophy serves as a framework for Christian *paideia* and is well showcased in the thought of Gregory.[21] It is driven by an emphasis of returning the soul to God.[22] This is the shared vision of the classical Greek thinkers and such important Christian thinkers as Gregory, Basil, and Macrina, as both aspired to generate a *paideia* that truly educates their respective communities. That portion of Rhee's conclusion "that we may know Him" can now be seen as the primary goal of any relationship shared between the books and the Book.

By way of admonition for those who teach in the setting of Christian higher education, there is a necessary vigilance in finding ways to articulate an intelligible theory of faith and learning integration and then put such a theory into practice as part of an entire institutional ethos. One place to begin in distinguishing the CLAU from the secular academy is by taking some inspiration from the early Christian thinkers who had an explicit vision that connected the books and the Book. It is in this sense that Rhee's notion of "the books and the Book" draws our attention to the most ancient of educational values, viz. the emergence of a genuine Christian *paideia* rooted in the reflections of the classical Greeks. With the added feature of "that we may know Him," a significant curricular statement with an essential *telos* is being made here in the context of the CLAU. That which is at stake is genuinely soul shaping and gives direction on a pathway to wisdom found in knowing Christ.

There is rich ore to be mined from such important early Christian figures as Origen, Gregory of Nyssa, Basil, and Macrina in building an intelligible understanding of Christian *paideia* rooted in what in modern parlance is called the liberal arts. It is against the backdrop of these salient thinkers that we can find a way to bring the thinking of the ancients forward

19. Ibid., 97–99.
20. Ibid., 98
21. Ibid.
22. Ibid., 99.

that generates a fresh and compelling vision of the integration of faith and learning. The *paideia* of the Greeks brought a deep and lasting influence on the way the theologians in the generations after the Apostles created a model for Christian education. Their work is worthy of our consideration in the contemporary CLAU. Our view is that Rhee agrees with our assessment of these matters given his love for the books and the Book. But he recognizes that the integration of faith and learning requires a humble, cautious, and painstaking process of constant dialog, given the troubled history of educational models that seek rapprochement between faith and learning.

The integration of faith and learning, as an educational philosophy, intentionally seeks to capitalize on the human inclination to create culture. In part, Christian *paideia* expresses itself in the vital mode of the CLAU. The educational ground the CLAU seeks to create is a synthesis of the faith-based instruction seen in the language of the "integration of faith and learning." Rhee's use of the phrase "the books and the Book" is a clear reflection of this sentiment. If this is right we look to Dr. Rhee's reference to "the books and the Book" as a means to contribute to the ongoing conversation about how faith and learning can be integrated in such places called CLAUs.

McIntyre, Hauerwas, and the Dis-Integration of Faith and Learning: Theology (Philosophy) and Disciplining the Disciplines

In his work, *God, Philosophy, and Universities*, Alasdair McIntyre complains that much of modern university education, for all its success, lives in the absence of any integrated and overall view of things.[23] Yet *paideia* is an integrative concept that helps find practical application in the way Christian liberal arts institutions organize their curriculums and deliver their degree programs. Hence, in the CLAU *paideia* is modified by the name Christian and its conception of God as an all determining reality. Christian *paideia* speaks of a reality that is one overseen by God in Christ and that which unifies the academic disciplines usually called the liberal arts. For McIntyre, this spells the end of the kind of specialization which separates and divides the disciplines in the modern university.

---

23. MacIntyre, *God, Philosophy, and Universities*, 16–18.

Christian *Paideia* and the Educational Vision of Song Nai Rhee

In a similar vein, Stanley Hauerwas wants to know just what the university is for and whom does it serve? If the university is to be a CLAU (though Hauerwas is quite uncomfortable with such institutions) it is to be a place that has its knowledges (academic disciplines) theologically disciplined.[24] Hauerwas argues that, in some sense, all that he has ever written supports the claim "that theology is a knowledge that should rightly be represented in the curriculums of a secular or church-sponsored university."[25] His overall project is to make the church capable of resisting knowledges, as they are proffered in the modern university, whose end is to make the church invisible.[26] He writes:

> The university is the great institution of legitimation in modernity whose task is to convince us that the way things are is the way things have to be. The specialization, what some describe as fragmentation, of the knowledges that constitute the curriculums of the modern university is crucial for the formation of people to be faithful servants of the status quo and, in particular, the modern nation state.[27]

Hauerwas' misgivings about the modern university are tempered by the hope that Christians might come to see that theology, understood as knowledge of God, is not restricted to "one field."[28] Rather, theology might serve as an integrative discipline that unifies all the disciplines, especially for "universities who owe their existence to the church."[29] Hauerwas' suggestions seem to be useful thought processes when we consider what the integration of faith and learning might look like in the CLAU. If Hauerwas is right, the CLAU then must ensure that all which is part of its curriculum is ordered by theology. Then the CLAU might well be on its way toward generating an interesting and intelligible paideia. In a cautious siding with John Milbank, Hauerwas warns that the very status of the secular university has become incoherent "because it has abandoned the theological task of studying that which is inimitably real."[30]

---

24. Hauerwas, *The State of the University*, 24.
25. Ibid., 23
26. Ibid., 4.
27. Ibid., 5.
28. Ibid., 7.
29. Ibid.
30. Ibid., 22.

With regard to a critique of contemporary university/college education, the respective analyses of Hauerwas and McIntyre come together in their discontent with the current curricular fragmentation in the university. Their often parallel diagnoses of the modern university merge into a singular claim that much can be solved by noting that theology and philosophy are just the right forms of academic inquiry to discipline the disciplines.[31] As McIntyre observes, "From the outset their (universities) forms of organization, their curricula, and their modes of teaching presuppose answers to questions that are central to the projects of theistic philosophical enquiry, questions about the relationships of philosophy both to theology and to the whole range of secular academic disciplines."[32] Of course, as McIntyre is aware, such a claim "...puts theists at odds with any purely secular understanding of such academic disciplines."[33] The kind of curricular fragmentation that McIntyre and Hauerwas are at pains to cure presents itself as a problem that makes academic disciplines (especially in the American university) autonomous and self-defining with no general requirement that students know anything about the other disciplines.[34]

In Rhee's view, such educational fragmentation is caused by a wedge driven between the books and the Book. Another feature of the Rhee heuristic that parallels Macintyre's assessment becomes apparent in that there should be a "concern for enquiry into the relationships between the disciplines" and a "conception of the disciplines as each contributing to a single shared enterprise."[35] Rhee's perspective is that academics who carry Christian convictions must insist on their rightful place at the table of the academy. But insistence is no guarantee that this place will be granted. Rather, Christian academics must be willing to submit their work to the usual protocols of intellectual rigor found in the disciplines of the liberal arts before seeking membership in the academy. To be credible, Christian liberal arts institutions cannot and must not fail on this matter. They must be willing to live in the tension of a pedagogical environment that both nurtures and challenges faith.

Without this kind of interdisciplinary approach to the disciplines, universities are more appropriately named "multiversities" or perhaps

---

31. Ibid., 49.
32. MacIntyre, *God, Philosophy, Universities*, 15.
33. Ibid.
34. Ibid., 16.
35. Ibid., 174.

Christian *Paideia* and the Educational Vision of Song Nai Rhee

"pluriversities" because they represent a kind of partitioned and fragmented pedagogy that occurs there.[36] McIntyre notes three ways in which the contemporary university has been successful, viz. in research, as providing the "prologue to specialization and professionalization" via its undergraduate programs, and the ironic phenomena of acquired wealth of the university and the increasing costs for those who attend the university.[37] However, for all its success, the university has lost any impetus into exploring the manner in which the disciplines are related to one another and how the disciplines may work toward a shared enterprise.[38] Such an enterprise should not be aimed at benefitting the economy or advancing the careers of students, in Macintyre's view. His admonition is that our conception of the university should be informed by our conception of the universe, one that works as a whole wherein the various disciplines are parts of an integrated system of enquiry, as opposed to "a multifarious set of assorted subject matters."[39] If the loss of integration is a problem in the research university, how much more would this be a problem for the CLAU that seeks to integrate faith and learning? The unfortunate effect of the loss of integration is that there is a kind of educational tribalism in the disciplines.[40] According to McIntyre, we begin to solve this problem by seeking to achieve a philosophical understanding of each of the disciplines and the relationship each discipline shares with the others.[41]

The problem of how the disciplines are to be disciplined remains as an enormous difficulty for the secular university. What arises is a kind of pedagogical "humpty dumpty" with no clear means of putting the pieces together again. Such a fracture between faith and learning represents an educational tragedy that needs to be cured by thoughtful reflection and action in the CLAU. But there is hazardous ground here since the CLAU may also inadvertently rupture the connection of faith and learning by becoming too dependent on educational models found in the secular university. The seductive quality of the cultural success of the secular university tempts those who lead in the CLAU to replicate the educational programs found in the secular arena. So called "marketable" programs are simply aped from

36. Ibid.
37. Ibid., 173–74.
38. Ibid., 174.
39. Ibid.
40. Ibid., 176.
41. Ibid., 175.

what is seen in the secular university. While CLAU's obviously need financial viability, there is the risk that the CLAU might become more beholding to the secular university, creating an educational environment that threatens its *paideia*.

In Macintyre's view, because theology and philosophy have lost their rightful place in the university (the first having been expelled and the latter being treated as one discipline among others) an important piece of raising questions about what is crucial for human flourishing is missing from the curricula.[42] McIntyre privileges philosophy and theology as integrative disciplines that make Christian *paideia* possible, and by inference create the grounds for an integration of faith and learning. For him, theology and philosophy are no longer just disciplines among the disciplines, but rather the unique means of bringing the disciplines together. These disciplines have the best resources to treat as axiomatic the claim that there is an underlying unity to the universe.[43] For McIntyre, philosophy is especially equipped to address the polarized status of the disciplines that traditionally comprise a university's overall curriculum. His concern is that even philosophy has fallen victim to a rampant ethos of specialization that separates biology from psychology, sociology from literature, history from business, and chemistry from anthropology, etc. Macintyre's argument is that philosophy is a discipline so configured that it could lead the way to a re-envisioning of how universities structure their curriculums. He argues that theology (which has no clear lines of demarcation with philosophy) as knowledge of God should be the educational net that holds the entire curriculum together. This makes sense given his Roman Catholic convictions regarding university degree programs. But as a point of concern, he adds that undergraduate education has become mere training ground for specialized graduate degree programs.[44]

The liberal arts as an educational vision are concerned with the investigation and study of the entirety of reality (the universe) via the mechanism of the university. As is readily seen, the term university is a cognate of universe. Just as universe is an idea or concept meant to capture the notion of a singular, unified reality, university is an instrument of learning that studies the one reality. Both are holistic in nature. Such is the central work of theology (and philosophy), at least as McIntyre interprets it.

42. Ibid., 175–76.
43. Ibid., 17.
44. Ibid.

Christian *Paideia* and the Educational Vision of Song Nai Rhee

Theology (and its handmaiden, philosophy) is a means of peace making and re-sacralizing a world that seems at war with God and that has been drained of the divine. Macintyre's Catholic sentiments may be interpreted as a discussion about the unity of nature and grace wherein we find the theology that lies behind the sacraments. In a like manner, the integration of faith and learning is another way of thinking about the way theology does the practical work of healing an open wound between the sacred and the secular, a wound largely created by the secular university. By our lights, the CLAU is strongly positioned to return theology to its rightful place as the queen of the sciences and to cure any rift that might exist between the books and the book.

Charles Taylor contributes to this conversation as he describes three forms of secularity that seemed to have flourished in the West, of which the modern university is a part. The first is found in the common institutions and practices reflected in a state that is free from its connection to a belief structure that excludes God[45] or have been "emptied of God."[46] The second is described as the falling off of religious belief and practices by the people who comprise the population of a state,[47] what might be seen as the ebbing of traditional religious activities commonly seen in churches, synagogues, and mosques. And yet a third form of secularity is observed by Taylor described as the conditions of belief in God (or a transcendent reality) that makes such belief merely one option among others, no more or less compelling than the other options. Taylor's analysis of secularity concerns itself with an attempt to discover how we have shifted from a society "in which it was virtually impossible to not believe in God, to one in which faith . . . is one possibility among others."[48] Formerly belief in God was "unchallenged and indeed, unproblematic" but is now "understood to be one option among others. . ."[49]

This final version of Taylor's analysis of secularity gives license to the prospect of a cultural "shrug of the shoulders," a cavalier "so what" as Christian educators strive to cast an educational philosophy that proffers the virtues of a covenant between faith and learning. Christian educators who strive to uphold the banner of a coherent means of integrating faith with

---

45. Taylor, *A Secular Age*, 1.
46. Ibid., 2.
47. Ibid.
48. Ibid., 3.
49. Ibid.

learning face the strong possibility of having their voices drowned out by a cacophony of culturally powerful secular institutions of higher learning. Assuming Taylor has correctly assessed the ways in which secularity has made its presence felt in our culture, all three versions of secularism noted by Taylor are difficult challenges for those who attempt to craft an intelligible vision of how faith and learning can be partnered in the educational mission of the CLAU.

The integration of the disciplines is a model or precursor to the integration of faith and learning. It is an apologetic that leads to a superior form of learning because the parts of the universe are seen in their connection to God, that the universe's unity and intelligibility can be adequately grasped. Such an approach creates the room necessary for a theistic comprehension of human beings that they may be fully comprehended. If faith and learning are to be genuinely integrated in the CLAU, such integration will have as its design a means to direct us to God.[50]

The expulsion of theology and the marginalization of philosophy in the secular academy in part leads to impoverished dialogue where those trained in a particular way tend to speak only to other like trained experts. The unfortunate result is that such an approach tends to "successfully exclude from the discussion all but their colleagues."[51] McIntyre observes that an attempt to understand the universe (a central project in philosophy) requires an acknowledgement which presupposes our dependence on God for our being.

Philosophy is then contoured in an Augustinian fashion that directs us toward God.[52] McIntyre recognizes that he will have to field objections to this view but is resolute in his claim that there has been a failure to understand how human beings are ultimately directed toward God.[53] In fact he acknowledges that what he has in mind may be overly ambitious because a spirit of cooperation between the disciplines is necessary for his educational vision to take root. Its only hope comes in first recognizing the integrative capacity of philosophy as it works as liaison between the disciplines. He rues the fact that even the most prestigious Catholic universities tend to copy prominent secular universities with little recognition

---

50. MacIntyre, *God, Philosophy, Universities*, 178–79.

51. Ibid., 176.

52. Ibid., 178.

53. Ibid., 179.

Christian *Paideia* and the Educational Vision of Song Nai Rhee

that something has gone very wrong.[54] The very existence of the CLAU carries an implied dissatisfaction with a form of education that is inadequate or falls short in some crucial ways. Some of these shortcomings have already been described above by Alasdair McIntyre in the emergence of the research university. Perhaps one of those points of dissatisfaction is seen in the fact that belief in God is no longer axiomatic.[55] Taylor complains that there has been a systematic crowding out of religious belief in our secular age.[56] He argues that a sense of fullness has been lost because of the advent secular thinking in culture of modernity in which we now live. Christian *paideia* in the CLAU creates the necessary room for an educational project that seeks to encounter this fullness of being. Taylor's description is that the place of fullness is to address human yearning.[57] Perhaps such thinking is what McIntyre has in mind when he describes his vision of education and the place of God in the university as an Augustinian project.

Knowing Christ as Sacramental Embodiment: the books and the Book "that we may know him"

> "What cannot be said must be passed over in silence."
> —Ludwig Wittgenstein

Without care the emphasis on the "books and the Book" may cause us to lose sight of the real *telos* (end, purpose, goal) of a vision that extols the educational virtues of the CLAU where, as we have argued, the integration faith and learning are best exhibited. That is, bringing the books and the book together in curricular relationship might be seen as an end unto itself. However, Rhee has already included the appropriate corrective for such a mistake by referencing the ultimate purpose of integrating faith and learning, viz. "that we may know Him." Hence, the focus on meshing the books and the book in a unified educational whole is not designed to singularly

---

54. Ibid.
55. Taylor, *A Secular Age*, 3.
56. Ibid., 4.
57. Ibid., 7–8.

to bring educational credibility to the CLAU in an environment where it is often discredited. Rather, the apex of such an educational practice is that Christians who pursue higher academics may know Christ. This is so because central to Christian *paideia* is the claim that God has spoken definitively and completely in the person of Jesus Christ. The guiding narrative for Christians is that "God (in the singular, not the plural) is the God of Jesus Christ." Integrating faith and learning, then, only become important if the educational aims of the CLAU are directed toward achieving a knowledge of the central person of this narrative.

There is a constellation of reasons as to why the integration of faith and learning is a notoriously nettlesome issue. Perhaps the prickly quality of how faith and learning are to be integrated can be somewhat reduced if it is first resolved that such a concept is not allowed to crystallize into a leaden religious dogma. Rather than framed as dogma, faith and learning are integrated in a way that naturally emerges from the entire life of the Christian academic. They are brought together as a key mode of what it means to live the Christian life. Hence, there is something contradictory in being a Christian scholar where faith and academic discipline are divided into separate categories of life. This danger emerges in the inevitable comparisons between the secular university and the CLAU. Unwittingly, the CLAU participates in a narrative that is not its own and thereby gives tacit permission, that is, by default, to the secular university to set the pedagogical agenda for universities everywhere. Such a failure on the part of the CLAU adds fuel and energy to an already de-sacralized world that happily splits faith and learning in a way that puts faith in the inferior position.

While "the books and the Book" may have a somewhat non-descript quality, its first meaning seems to carry the notion of a love for the world and its books since these contain the ideas forming human culture. As might be expected, there continues to be well intended attempts to generate a penetrating analysis of just what it means to say that the integration of faith and learning is central to the educational ideals of the CLAU. To this point, such explanations are unsatisfying, leaving the reader still wanting greater clarity about the nature of the integration of faith and learning.

But how are the circumstances which potentially force the CLAU to surrender its unique vision in the world of post-secondary education to be avoided? What are we left with as we try to wrap our minds around the meaning of "the integration of faith and learning"? Where can we turn to gain some clarity about the core meaning of faith and learning integration?

Christian *Paideia* and the Educational Vision of Song Nai Rhee

Do we simply acquiesce to the impenetrable quality of faith and learning integration because its very nature defies being defined? With a cautious "yes" in mind, a hopeful possibility may be found in the reflections of Terence Cuneo's essay, *Ritual Knowledge*. Here Cuneo argues that knowledge of a religious sort means "being in rapport" with another and not "acquaintance with an object."[58] Cuneo's claim is that being in rapport with another then is in some sense a ritual activity, perhaps described as sacramental in nature.

In other terms, ritual knowledge may be described as personal knowledge, i.e. knowledge that is not a sterile, clinical sense of knowing as is the case with, say, scientific knowledge. Rather it is the kind of knowledge that involves intimacy, or what Cuneo refers to as being in rapport. In a strikingly similar kind of argument, Kierkegaard claims that bringing "God to light objectively" is "in all eternity impossible."[59] This is so because "God is a subject" just as we are subjects. The possibility of rapport entails humans as subjects relating to God as a subject. Kierkegaard calls our subjective knowledge of God a "God-relationship" and when such knowledge exists believers are in a state of "inwardness" or subjectivity.[60] Kierkegaard refers to human beings as "existing individuals" who, as subjects, can only "know" God in a religious sense, who is also a subject. He extends his argument to show that any attempt at objective knowledge of God is an "approximation-process" that amounts to idolatry.[61] If the *telos* of the Christian is to "know Him," as in knowing Christ, then the connection between Cuneo and Kierkegaard is made evident by their varying terminology that describes a singular concept. That is, ritual knowledge and subjective knowledge come together in the terms of rapport and inwardness to describe what Rhee hopes for in Christian higher education when he points to the aspiration of "that we may know Him."

Adapted to the interests of the integration of faith learning, Cuneo's argument helps us see what it means to use the step-ladder of the "books and the Book" that we may know Christ in the sense of "being in rapport" with him. It must be confessed that the linguistics of "the integration of

58. Cuneo, "Ritual Knowledge," 368.
59. Kierkegaard, *Concluding Unscientific Postscript*, 178.
60. Ibid.
61. Ibid., 180. Kierkegaard anticipates Martin Buber's *I and Thou* as another means to describe what it means for humans to be involved in an intimate relationship with the divine.

faith and learning" does not wear its meaning on its face,[62] especially if this language takes on the status of a creed or religious dogma. But the integration of faith and learning has real depth of meaning if it is understood liturgically or sacramentally because it brings us into rapport with the person of Jesus Christ vis a vis a lifeless doctrine.

If these reflections are accurate, then the enigmatic quality of the integration of faith and learning is one of great virtues. We do not propose that the above thinking clears away all of the clutter that has collected around the topic of faith and learning integration. In fact, the integration of faith and learning has a certain ineffable quality that adds to its mystery. The interface between faith and learning is one of those many human endeavors that is known but cannot be explained, at least in some complete or satisfying sense. The heart of Cuneo's argument provides a lens that helps us understand the importance of "that we may know Him." By extension, the meaning of "the integration of faith and learning" acquires additional clarity through the instructional activity of the scholar-teacher in the classrooms of the CLAU. Rather than being *explained*, the integration of faith and learning is *observed* by students in the CLAU who see their professors in action, i.e. professors embody in incarnational fashion the very educational value that is said to be key to the ethos of the CLAU. Faith and learning integration is not a theological dogma but is rather incarnated in the lives of those who teach in CLAUs. In this sense faith and learning is incarnational, and hence, liturgical (or in Cuneo's language, "ritual").

We are committed to the view that the integration of faith and learning must be embodied in the lives of those who teach in the CLAU. It is the ground or environment wherein the Christian academic refuses to live a hyphenated life that splits her academic training from her faith commitments. Seeing the integration of faith and learning in this sacramental and liturgical sense provides the avenue that ultimately honors and commends the life of Dr. Song Nai Rhee as one who consistently carries this incarnational model of Christian higher education. By way of analogy and extension, just as we know God by knowing Christ, it might be said that we know the meaning of the integration of faith and learning by knowing such people as Dr. Song Nai Rhee, who is the consummate Christian scholar.

This is why the academic and religious life of Dr. Song Nai Rhee is a compelling showcase of a powerful academic preparation coupled with a heartfelt commitment to the Christian faith. He is the embodiment of a life

---

62. Cuneo, "Ritual Knowledge," 368.

Christian *Paideia* and the Educational Vision of Song Nai Rhee

that is compelling because of his recognition that the Christian faith is not made stronger by isolating itself from a deep involvement and interaction with the world at large. Rhee's own academic training is demonstrative of a devout person who has earned two PhDs in the academic areas of biblical studies and archaeology, making him the ideal Christian scholar. Rhee readily sees that biblical studies and archaeology go about their work in quite different ways, but there is no reason to build artificial and unnecessary barriers between these two academic disciplines. For Rhee, trained experts in biblical studies and archaeology (as with all academic disciplines) should be governed by a philosophy of education that links faith and learning in a liberal arts college or university. Rhee then is the classic man of letters whose wisdom and educational training has equipped him to think deeply about how the integration of faith and learning can be best understood without being explained.

Concluding Reflections

In keeping with the intent of the entire festschrift our essay celebrates the life and scholarly activity of Dr. Song Nai Rhee, particularly because his life exemplifies a deeply held conviction about the importance of the integration of faith and learning in the CLAU. Our central concern is to give due honor and respect to one who has thought creatively and worked tirelessly to uphold the importance of integrating faith and learning in the unique context of the CLAU. Rhee's remarkable 60 year connection to NCU is one where he has lead by example by translating the words of "the books and the Book, that we may know Him" into action. For Rhee, these words have never been mere slogan-making. Equally so, it is important for CLAU's to never leave the impression that the "integration of faith and learning" is merely an empty platitude, employed simply because it sounds "sexy." But it is rather a kind of covenantal promise made to prospective students and parents. This promise takes the form of ensuring that the respective CLAU will make ongoing and lively debate about the integration of faith and learning an institutional priority. At the forefront of institutional identity is an ethos that continues the demanding work of bringing faith and learning into a cooperative arrangement.

Song Nai Rhee's affirmation of the "the books and the Book" is a tacit recognition that the liberal arts (the books) play a necessary though not sufficient role in the truly educated student who is trained in the CLAU.

Rhee's view seems to be a kind of foil against any theological work that cleaves the marriage between the books and the Book. A modest approach is to take Rhee's insight as a steadying force that maintains the intimacy between the books and the Book. As a concept, the integration of faith and learning inherently proclaims for itself a certain educational gravitas that deepens and strengthens one's relationship with Christ. Part of this gravitas serves to distinguish the CLAU from the secular university. Such a distinction requires a clear articulation of the integration of faith and learning. To reach this level of educational quality requires that the relationship between the books and the Book be kept intact.

Song Nai Rhee was and remains an iconic figure at NCU in part because of his deep commitment to the integration of faith and learning. With his arrival at NCC nearly six decades ago he began an illustrious career as a student, teacher, and a member of upper administration. Even after his retirement in 2000, Dr. Rhee continues his heartfelt commitment to the success and development of NCU. As current faculty members at NCU, we are humbled and pleased to have written these words of commendation and recognition honoring the work of Dr. Song Nai Rhee. We are proud to have our teaching careers overlap with such a remarkable figure. As now seasoned faculty, who have spent the bulk of our teaching lives at NCC/NCU, we see our work as a continuation of Rhee's legacy begun so many years ago and hope that our younger faculty colleagues at NCU might take inspiration from the enduring quality of his work.

Bibliography

Bertram, Georg. "*Paideia*." In *TDNT* 5:596–625.
Cuneo, Terence. "Ritual Knowledge." *Faith and Philosophy* 31 (2014) 365–85.
Hauerwas, Stanley. *The State of the University*. Malden, MA: Blackwell, 2007.
Jaeger, Werner. *Early Christianity and Greek Paideia*. Cambridge: Harvard University Press, 1961.
Kierkegaard, Soren. *Concluding Unscientific Postscript*. Translated by David Swenson and Walter Lowrie. Princeton: Princeton University Press, 1941.
McIntyre, Alasdair. *God, Philosophy, Universities: A Selective History of the Catholic Philosophical Tradition*. New York: Rowan & Littlefield, 2011.
Taylor, Charles. *A Secular Age*. Cambridge: Harvard University Press, 2007.

2

Spirituality, Ancient Traditions, and the Modern Workplace

Michael Kennedy

MY VOCATIONAL LIFE HAS been expressed in two key fashions: as an ordained clergyman who spent 21 years in the Navy as a chaplain (MDiv, Yale) and as an academic with an earned doctorate (DBA, Nova Southeastern University) in the co-disciplines of business and management. I am recently retired (2011) from Northwest Christian University as a professor where I taught a range of courses for both undergraduate and graduate students who aspired to their own careers as successful businessmen and businesswomen. For me, this blend of theological reflection and business practice has created an intense interest in how matters of spirituality might find their way into the modern workplace. Hence, this essay explores some of the salient possibilities of extending spirituality (and even matters of faith) from the realm of that which is often viewed as private to the public arena generally and the workplace specifically.

My interest in spirituality is underpinned by a view that when we are thinking about matters that go to the core of our being, viz. spirituality, it is impossible not to bring such identities to the variety of contexts where we live our lives. If we are driven by a set of core values and beliefs that are determinative of our being, we cannot help but express these values in our interactions with family members, friends, neighbors, and co-workers.

For example, who we are as parents and employees is governed by a single character crafted from a body of demanding spiritual values. It is the highest form of hypocrisy to turn these values on and off because the contexts of life might demand it in the name of comfort. Such an approach to that which we have deemed as values transforms us into creatures of expediency as opposed to that of principle.

The spiritual values to which I adhere arise from my Christian convictions. While I am never entitled to be impositional with these convictions, they are necessarily at play in all the contexts where my character is on display. They are a natural extension of who I am as a human being and are not to be "checked at the door" when I enter the various arenas of which my life is composed. Hence, in what follows I discuss and assess the matter of spirituality and the ways in which it finds a natural setting in the modern workplace. My views are held together by the conviction that humans are at bottom spiritual beings who are truly at home when their core values are given room to develop and flourish.

The Matter of a Paradigm Shift

"Paradigm shift" is a borrowed concept finding its origin in the thinking of Thomas Kuhn's influential book, *The Structure of Scientific Revolutions*. Primarily for the purposes of scientific method and discovery, Kuhn defines paradigm as standing for "the entire constellation of beliefs, values, techniques, and so on by the members of a given community."[1] George Goodman (writing under the pseudonym "Adam Smith") expands Kuhn's definition stating that a paradigm is "a shared set of assumptions" and because we are in the middle of it, ". . .it is hard to imagine any other paradigm."[2] Joel Barker develops the notion of paradigm even further by noting that it is "a set of rules and regulations (written and unwritten) that . . . establishes or defines boundaries"; and ". . . tells you how to behave inside the boundaries in order to be successful."[3] Barker observes that the definition allows us to talk of paradigms and paradigm shifts in fields other than science.[4]

Kuhn also emphasizes the manner in which scientific revolutions interact with scientific development. He writes that "scientific revolutions are

1. Kuhn, *The Structure of Scientific Revolutions*, 175.
2. Smith, 19
3. Barker, *Paradigms*, 32.
4. Ibid.

Spirituality, Ancient Traditions, and the Modern Workplace

inaugurated by a growing sense . . . that an existing paradigm has ceased to function adequately in the exploration of an aspect of nature to which that paradigm itself previously led the way."[5] These revolutions, which Kuhn calls paradigm shifts,[6] result in a new paradigm being accepted.

Such a shift is readily seen when Copernicus' discoveries supplanted the model espoused by Ptolemy, moving from a geocentric to a heliocentric vision of the cosmos. This shift in thinking caused a major realignment in science as well as the entire fabric of society. Copernicus' (and later Newton's) cosmological image was so pervasive it penetrated every domain of society. In fact this scientific paradigm was so dominant that a so called "objective knowledge" took over to the point that all truth was known through experimentation and controlled observation in a way that placed all truth outside the human individual.

At the beginning of the twentieth century, this understanding began to change as science itself underwent a paradigm shift. The discoveries of Albert Einstein and Max Planck, dealing with the speed of light and the smallest particles, led to the development of quantum physics. This new area of physics depicted a world that was strikingly different from the world as seen in classical Newtonian physics. In light of Kuhn's original claims, other sciences such as chemistry, biology, ecology, and psychology have also undergone significant paradigm shifts. The totalizing impact of paradigm shifts in nearly all areas of human endeavor even includes scientific attention being given to the "inner experiences of individuals, including intuition, emotions, creativity, and spirit. . ." as opposed to a form of science that focuses on the senses alone.[7]

This current shift has been compared in importance to the Copernican one. Wheatley observes that modern organizations are primarily Newtonian in nature.[8] Unfortunately, in such organizations, there is an emphasis on charts that depict the business as though it were a machine. People are organized into roles and placed on the charts as parts of the machine. But in this new world, the machine has disappeared and in its place are relationships.

---

5. Kuhn, *The Structure of Scientific Revolutions*, 92.
6. Ibid., 66.
7. Ray, "Introduction," in *The New Paradigm in Business*, 2.
8. Wheatley, *Leadership and the New Sciences*, 2.

A Paradigm Shift in Business

When a paradigm shift occurs in any area of human concern, the impact is far reaching as noted in the examples above. Management is not excluded from the changes that are demanded when a paradigm shift occurs. Neal writes, "many people in the management education field have been sensing and discussing a paradigm shift in management theory and practice in the past few years."[9] Further, Neal notes that this shift includes a shift from competition to collaboration, an increased awareness of employee and customer needs. For her "there is a movement away from a theoretical approach that attempted to be 'value-free' to an approach that emphasizes employee, manager, and organizational values as critical to organizational effectiveness."[10] She sees this new paradigm as shifting the focus from machines and clockwork mechanisms to a search for meaning in the midst of a turbulent time. This search includes an increasing interest in spirituality, in general, and including spirituality in the workplace.

Motivated by the Spirit

Mary Parker Follett's views coming from works produced in 1918 and 1924 represent a paradigm shift away from what is often called scientific management. In scientific management optimal production is created by a strict "division of labor, with each worker performing endlessly, under close supervision, the same repetitious task."[11] Follett's views have re-emerged as "applicable for modern managers dealing with rapid changes in today's global environment. Her approach to leadership stresses the importance of people rather than engineering techniques."[12] Follett's work became a somewhat ubiquitous voice against scientific management for the remainder of the twentieth century.

In this sense, Follett provides an interesting point of departure in a discussion about how people are motivated in the context of the workplace. Her work provides the means to shed light on better alternatives to scientific management. To move this discussion forward we turn to Abraham Maslow and a few individuals who followed him in their thinking about

---

9. Ibid., 121.
10. Graham, *Mary Parker-Follett*.
11. Ibid.
12. Daft, *Management*, 49.

human motivation. These individuals include Douglas McGregor, Frederick Herzberg, and Peter Senge.

Maslow's hierarchy of needs has near iconic and unquestioned status in the western world of psychology and sociology. Beginning with the most basic need of humans, viz. the physiological, moved upwardly to other needs described in ascending order as safety, love, esteem, and self-actualization. The list of needs are in reality motivators of behavior with each need serving as a prompt that helps people aspire to meeting the next need in the rungs of the ladder above. Maslow translated his own study of the relationship between human behavior and motivation into the work situation, providing insights into the art of management.

Douglas McGregor examined Maslow's hierarchy of needs, observing that assumptions about human motivation needed to be at the core of any theory of management. He viewed Maslow as providing some of the required basic ideas about human motivation. McGregor's work, inspired by Maslow, pits him against the idea of labor espoused by the scientific management theorists. Hence, McGregor has what he needs to proffer a new theory of management in terms of human resources. His efforts strive to push away styles of management that depend on direction and control.[13]

Frederick Herzberg continues Maslow's theory in many important ways by steering the latter's thinking away from a general sense of human needs to one that focuses on the workplace specifically. Herzberg theorized self-actualization (as construed by Maslow) and job satisfaction would be met in the workplace when such matters as recognition for accomplishment, challenging work, increased job responsibility, and opportunities for growth were given strong attention by management.

Late in life even Maslow (and in connection with Herzberg) recognized the possibility of going beyond self-actualization. In language that refers to what he calls Theory Z, Maslow employs such spiritually sounding terms as "transpersonal," "transcendent," and "transhuman"[14] which could meet the "metaneeds" of people.[15]

Peter Senge belongs to the tradition established by Maslow because he argues that when it comes to organizations and their systems, they must be treated as a "discipline for seeing wholes" which provides the

---

13. Hersey, et.al., *Management of Organizational Behavior*, 68.
14. Maslow, *Motivation and Personality*, 275.
15. Ibid., 274.

capacity for "seeing interrelationships rather than things."[16] The building blocks of Senge's thinking results in a required spiritual growth and seeing "one's life as a creative work, living life from a creative as opposed to reactive viewpoint" (p. 141).[17] Quoting Bill Obrien, president of Hanover insurance, Senge brings Obrien's thinking alongside his own by noting, "our traditional hierarchical organizations are not designed to provide for people's higher order needs, self-respect and self-actualization. The ferment in management will continue until organizations begin to address these needs, for all employees."[18] Jacobson notes the broader appeal of Senge's thinking by seeing it as relevant to many other disciplines.[19] When seen in its most robust sense Senge's vision, ". . .taken to its full power" causes issues of spirituality to come to the forefront, "consciously or not."[20] If Jacobson's analysis is right, that which is spiritual is nearly unavoidable for human beings. Our highest aspirations are best termed as our yearning for spirituality and that we are somehow less than human if such yearnings are not met or actualized.

Work and Spirituality in Modern and Ancient Settings

Attention is now directed to the fact that an interest in spirituality in the workplace is nothing new but is demonstrative of that which is being rediscovered. In what follows two ancient forms of spiritualty, viz. the Benedictine Rule and Celtic Spiritualty, will be gleaned for their applications in the modern workplace. After assessing these ancient forms of the spiritual life an investigation of Max Weber's thinking will be brought to a point of comparison and contrast with Michael Novak and his reflections on the spiritual life from a modern Roman Catholic's viewpoint.

St. Benedict

In the mid-sixth century CE, St. Benedict developed his Rule to provide guidance and structure to the many monasteries that were founded at that

16. Senge, *The Fifth Discipline*, 68.
17. Ibid., 141.
18. Ibid., 140.
19. Ibid., 40.
20. Ibid., 44.

Spirituality, Ancient Traditions, and the Modern Workplace

time. His Rule lasted virtually unchanged for almost 1,500 years. Today, more than 1,400 communities of Benedictine and Cistercian men and women live this rule, and there are thousands of lay people who also follow as much of the rule as they can in the midst of their busy lives.

The rule that Benedict proffered wove together into one whole the entire life of the monks, including their contribution to the community of work. In chapter 48 of the rule, Benedict states, "Idleness is an enemy of the soul. Therefore, the brothers should be occupied according to the schedule in either manual labor or holy reading."[21] He continues by describing the overall day of the monk as one that intertwines work and prayer so as to establish a rhythm. This dynamic balance of forces allows each monk to strive to be his best self within the life of the community. In this way Benedict lays the groundwork for seeing the desirability of spiritual practices in the workplace. "What we can learn from the Rule is that the sense of God's presence can be mediated through daily work and not destroyed by it."[22]

The influence of Benedict's Rule is not limited just to monasteries of the Church. In 1916 Henri Fayol published his General and Industrial Management (in French, translated into English in 1949) in which he outlines his fourteen functions of management. There is significant similarity in the emphasis of Fayol's system and Benedict's Rule. It is possible that Fayol had studied Benedict's Rule since he was educated at a missionary school in La Voulte, France, and his funeral service was held in the church of Sainte-Clotilde.[23]

These events assume importance when it is considered that "Henri Fayol's approach to administration more closely reflects the assumptions of theory Y, rather than theory X."[24] This is especially seen in his principle of *esprit de corps* and the atmosphere that established his functions and principles. These principles and functions make room for the development of the whole person.

Celtic Spirituality

If there is one people that believe in the unity of all of life it was the early Christian Celts. DeWaal points out that "these Celtic people lived quite

---

21. St. Benedict, *Benedict's Rule*, 86.
22. DeWaal, *The Celtic Way of Prayer*, 105.
23. Wren, personal correspondence, 8/15/1997.
24. Jones, et.al., *Contemporary Management*, 50.

naturally and quite unselfconsciously in a state of prayer whose daily and yearly rhythm was dictated…by the demands of a hard working existence."[25] Their prayer life grew out of their life itself and with its work and daily "humdrum" existence. For them there was not work time and personal time, but it was all of a piece. DeWaal states that "praying is not associated with going to church. Praying and living were not set apart, distinct."[26]

As a consequence, there is a sense of "sacredness of the earth and of all that grows in it, . . . an awareness that heaven is not far from us, (and) that in our work and in our sleep we are accompanied by heavenly powers."[27] Many of the daily prayers from the Celts reflect these characteristics and create images in words that draw us into their celebration of joy in the beauty of God's creation. But those who live in such close contact with nature know that along with the light there comes the dark, and along with the beauty comes the pain and agony found in a harsh world, reflected in the agony of the cross.

An example of these thoughts is contained in the following words of a Morning Prayer:

> Thanks be to Thee, Jesus Christ,
> Who brought'st me up from the last night,
> To the gladsome light of the this day,
> Through the blood Thou didst shed for me.
> Praise be to Thee, O God, forever,
> For the blessings Thou didst bestow on me-
> My food, my speech, my work, my health.[28]

Indeed, all the little chores of the day are dressed in prayer, from getting the fire started to sowing the fields to enjoying a banquet. The following are a sample of those types of prayers.

> I will kindle my fire this morning
> In the presence of the holy angels of heaven,
> In the presence of Ariel of the loveliest form,
> In the presence of Uriel of the myriad charmes.[29]

25. DeWaal, *God under the Roof*, 35.
26. DeWaal, *The Celtic Way of Prayer*, 72.
27. Allchin and DeWaal, 14–15.
28. Carmichael, *Celtic Invocations*, 39.
29. Allchin and DeWaal, *Daily Readings and Prayers*, 38.

Spirituality, Ancient Traditions, and the Modern Workplace

> I will go out to sow the seed,
> In name of Him who gave it growth;
> I will place my front in the wind,
> And throw a gracious handful on high.[30]

> I would like to have the men of Heaven
> In my own house:
> With vats of good cheer
> Laid out for them.
> I would like a great lake of beer
> For the King of Kings,
> I would like to be watching Heaven's family
> Drinking it through all eternity.[31]

It is in these blessings and prayers that it can be seen that the Christian Celts did feel a distinct interconnection with all they did. For this people, all of one's experiences were part of the ongoing quality of creation.

Max Weber

Of course it was not just the ancients who saw the need for a full integration of all aspects of their lives. Such views are also evidenced in the Protestant reformers who viewed their life's work as a calling, i.e. a vocation in its original sense. Perhaps Max Weber's classic study, *The Protestant Work Ethic and the Spirit of Capitalism*, best represents the perspective that all jobs are a calling. Weber alludes to Martin Luther and John Calvin on the common understanding of working in the world and the impact this attitude had on capitalism.

Weber's analysis engages the Roman Catholic position, as he saw it, as having two segments or classes of society, viz. the majority of the people (laity) who were the sinful masses and the monastic orders (clergy) who prayed on their behalf. According to Weber, "The only way of living acceptably to God was not to surpass the worldly morality in monastic asceticism, but solely through the fulfillment of the obligations imposed upon the individual by his position in the world. That was his calling."[32] R. H. Tawney

---

30. DeWaal, *God under the Roof*, 63.
31. Allchin and DeWaal, *Daily Readings and Prayers*, 58.
32. Weber, *The Protestant Work Ethic*, 80.

comments on Weber's view of work by noting that the latter saw "it as a spiritual end, for in it alone can the soul find health."[33]

Michael Novak

Novak (1993) takes up the Catholic position as a rejoinder against Weber's view. He thinks Weber has it right in the sense that our work has a religious underpinning.[34] Novak entitles his work as *The Catholic Ethic and the Spirit of Capitalism*, directly echoing Weber's title. Novak's purpose is to show that Weber's work actually assesses a narrow slice of Protestant practice that is found in the Puritans and not necessarily all of Protestantism.[35] Further, Novak argues in favor of capitalism by showing that Catholic theology serves to correct and enhance the larger spirit of capitalism. His point is to show that religion generally has impacted the development of capitalism in ways that can be attributed to both Catholicism and Protestantism and that such influence continues to this day.

Spirituality and Development in Organizations

When people come to work, they bring their values, their attitudes, their desires, and their spirituality. Until recently, those who write and think about organizational development have often failed to recognize these features of human life. Here again it is clear that a paradigm shift may be in the offing. What was previously regarded as too personal or irrelevant has begun to appear in the literature that discusses spiritualty in the workplace. In light of this development what is seen next reflects on a sampling of authors who write and speak to this issue. They are a family of thinkers who represent a logical extension of those discussed above in the writing of Maslow, McGregor, and Herzberg.

Those who enrich the conversation about spirituality in the workplace are Peter Vaill, Robert Greenleaf, Max Depree, Ken Blanchard, and Wayne Alderson. Each, in his own way, and with differently nuanced versions of spirituality, examine the means by which a paradigm shift is underway when spirituality becomes part and parcel to the world of business. For

---

33. Tawney, *Religion and the Rise of Capitalism*, 201.
34. Novak, *The Catholic Ethic*, 34.
35. Ibid., 7.

Spirituality, Ancient Traditions, and the Modern Workplace

instance, Vaill[36] uses the metaphor of "white water" to describe the chaos and turmoil of modern culture that extends into organizations. "White water" leads to confusion and generates a palpable meaninglessness[37] especially for leaders in an organization. Overcoming meaninglessness is a major theme in Vaill's most recent book, entitled *Spirited Leading and Learning*. Here he argues that organizations need to pay attention to the spiritual condition of their leaders.[38]

Robert Greenleaf's contributions to this conversation are famously known in his work on servant leadership. Greenleaf's Quaker roots are evident as he argues via quiet insistence for the presence of the spiritual in all things leads to a holistic understanding of work, personal development and shared decision making. . ."[39] His use of Herman Hesse's novel, *Journey to the East*, reveals an affinity for a leader, as seen in the figure of Leo, for the one who serves as a leader incognito. That is, he does not fit the usual paradigm of a leader who rules by assertive authority, but he leads because he first serves. Greenleaf's Christian convictions rise to the surface by his use of the passage in Matthew's (20:26–28) gospel (NIV) when Jesus tells his disciples, "Whoever wants to become great among you must be your servant, and whoever wants to be first must be your slave, just as the Son of Man did not come to be served, but to serve."

Max Depree credits Greenleaf with his insights about servant leadership. *In Leading Without Power*, Depree argues that if leaders lead without formal power, people will follow because they sense the commitment of their leaders. Such a claim is supported by a perspective that sees leaders as belonging to their people and as expressive of the notion of "the people I serve"[40] as a sign of true leadership. In a similar line of thinking Ken Blanchard proffers the view that it is people who ultimately in the organizational environment. In such a scenario people are set free to be genuine human beings in an atmosphere of caring.

Finally, in *Theory R Management* written by Alderson and McDonnell, we find the last example of the tradition begun by Maslow. The subtitle of the book reveals its basic concern, viz. "How to utilize the value of the person; Leadership principles of love, dignity, and respect." Their approach

---

36. Vaill, *Rediscovering the Soul of Business*, 2.
37. Vaill, *Management as a Performing Art*, 43.
38. Vaill, *Spirit Leading and Learning*, 218.
39. Lee and Zemke, *The Search for Spirit in the Workplace*, 22.
40. Depree, *Leading without Power*, 71.

flows directly from the foregoing theories and gets its name from the five "R's" that compose this theory. These five concepts are summarized by the authors: "When the fundamental motivation and guideline is doing what is right and the fundamental principle is building good *relationships* and the fundamental goal is bringing about *reconciliation* and the fundamental response on the part of everyone is *responsibility*, the by-product will be positive *results* for all persons involved."[41] Like Greenleaf's perspective, Theory R management is person centered. Alderson and McDonell note, "the Theory R leader takes on the garb of a servant and understands that by giving the self to serve employees, coworkers, and family members, power is not lost but gained."[42]

Cautions and Concerns

Of course, not everyone agrees that being open to spirituality in the workplace is a good thing. In a spiritually and religiously pluralistic society like ours, with its strong emphasis on the separation of church and state, there is the worry of "religion seeping into secular institutions, especially a corporate one" (Conlin, 1999, p. 154).[43] This separation often leads to the attitude that thoughts and feelings about spirituality are or should be "undiscussable" in secular organizations.[44] One of the fears in this regard concerns the possibility of "proselytizing about religion or using spiritual beliefs to exclude others,"[45] which is contrary to the concept of inclusion. There is also the fear that there is a "conspiracy proselytizing everyone into thinking alike."[46]

Part of the above set of concerns is the fear that "the boundary between the personal and the professional is being breached without any thought being given to the consequences."[47] Braham interviewed eight CEOs about their beliefs and practices. These eight individuals, who all practice their faith in their jobs, echo the thoughts expressed by one of the interviewees,

---

41. Alderson and McDonnell, *Theory R Management*, 34. Emphasis in the original.
42. Ibid., 135.
43. Conlin, "Religion in the Workplace," 154.
44. Mirvis, "Soul Work in Organizations, 202.
45. Ibid.
46. Conlin, "Religion in the Workplace," 156.
47. Ibid.

Spirituality, Ancient Traditions, and the Modern Workplace

viz. John Beckett, who said, "I want to be known as spiritual, not religious."[48] But in the same article, Laura Nash points out the CEOs are conflicted with a "very large discomfort" about their visibility. They worry about being too public, since it "either gets cynical or runs the danger of creating an abuse of power. It can be misinterpreted as proselytizing."[49]

Such a concern is not an idle worry. Lee and Zemke note that "spirituality has proved to be an explosive issue for trainers in recent years."[50] And these issues have often led to complaints. Conlin states in *Newsweek* that the "Equal Opportunity Commission reports a 29 percent spike since 1992 in the number of religious-based discrimination charges, making those the third-fastest growing claim, after sexual harassment and disability."[51] Hence, the negative repercussions arising from the good intent of infusing spirituality in the workplace are far reaching.

Perhaps the strongest criticism of the spirituality in the workplace movement comes from the management guru, Tom Peters. In a syndicated column in April 1993, Peters expressed concern for the growing enthusiasm for workplace spirituality. In the column, titled "Spiritual Talk has No Place in Secular Corporations," he writes:

> When the talk turns to the spiritual side of leadership, I mostly want to run. It should be enough if I work like hell, respect my peers, customers, and suppliers, and perform with verve, imagination, efficiency, and good humor. Please don't ask me to join the Gregorian chant Club, too.[52]

Peters spoke in favor of empowerment but noted that when imagination and curiosity, "let's leave the Bible, the Koran, and facile talk of spiritual leaders at home."[53] In speaking with Lee and Zemke for their 1993 article, he was more outspoken, saying "when you cross the line between the secular and the spiritual you're edging up to something that bugs be." He also graphically expressed that the idea of a corporation taking on the role of a religious institution "makes me want to puke."[54]

---

48. Ibid., 108.
49. Ibid., 49.
50. Lee and Zemke, "The Search for Spirit in the Workplace," 26.
51. Conlin, "Religion in the Workplace," 154.
52. Renesch and Defoore, eds. *The New Bottom Line*, 13.
53. Ibid., 13.
54. Lee and Zemke, The Search for Spirit in the Workplace, 26.

There are, of course, those who see anything that takes workers away from the job as detrimental to the organization. Alfred Batton, a sales manager, quoted by Andy Cohen, said, "I don't really care if this stuff helps anyone get through the day. Any time they're spending meditating or doing whatever they're doing is time not spent with customers."[55]

Renesch quotes William George, CEO of Medtronic, Inc., responding to Peters says, "Spiritual leadership in the workplace has nothing to do with church or religion. . . . At Medtronic we don't mix religion and business, but we certainly do not shy away from the spiritual side of our work and the deeper mission to save lives."[56] Renesch also responded to Peters by saying, "most advocates of spiritual principles for the workplace clearly distinguish between religion and spiritual, something Peters doesn't seem to grasp."[57] The distinction between a religious and a spiritual focus does seem to lead to confusion. Renesch responds a second time to Peters by mentioning the authors who support bringing the spirit into the workplace, such as James Autry, Max Depree, and Peter Senge. He queries Peters with, "Are you opposing the imposition of religious dogma and practices on workers who feel the need to comply to protect their jobs? If this . . . is your contention, I argue that you are confusing spiritual values with religious structures."[58]

Other writers as well have responded to Peters and his concerns. For example, Ian Mitroff wrote to Renesch saying,

> It is amazing the lengths to which we humans will go in order to deny and avoid the topic of spirituality. For Tom Peters, spirituality is equivalent to religion. . . Religion is only one of a number of institutions that have tried, often unsuccessfully, to make spirituality their central concern and mission. I do not see how organizations can function as a high level and truly meet the 'ethical needs and wants' of all stakeholders unless they learn to grapple seriously with spirituality.'[59]

Paralleling this form of thinking Mitroff and Denton in *A Spiritual Audit of Corporate America* argue that many organizations are taking a "perilous path" by separating matters of spirituality from the workplace.[60]

55. Cohen, "The Guiding Light," 47.
56. Renesch and Defoore, eds., *The New Bottom Line*, 17.
57. Ibid.
58. Renesch and Defoore, eds., *The New Bottom Line*, 25.
59. Mitroff, *A Spiritual Audit of Corporate America*, 27
60. Ibid., 7

They argue that it is by acknowledging the soul that organizations prepare themselves for the next millennium.[61]

Colby, in her 1998 article in the Los Angeles Times, addresses the issue of the lost spiritual dimension at work. She notes that there are concerns voiced by some with whom she talked that introducing spirituality into the workplace may be a means to "exploit employees." She responds by noting, "Companies that want to attract and keep good employees must also begin to incorporate spiritual values into their own management practices."

A compelling overview of this subject is found in Ashmos' and Duchon's study of spirituality at work. They write:

> Spirituality at work, despite religious imagery, is not about religion or conversion, or about getting people to accept a belief system. Rather, it is about employees who understand themselves as spiritual beings whose souls need nourishment at work. It is about experiencing a sense of purpose and meaning found, for example, in the job design literature, which emphasizes finding meaning in the performance of tasks. Spirituality is also people experiencing a sense of connectedness to one another and to their workplace community.[62]

While the concerns raised by such persons as Peters and Cohen have validity, to shy away from addressing the soul and its relation to the workplace for fear of conflict is to cause employees to bring only a part of themselves to work. The possibility of unleashing the creativity and commitment of workers who are one hundred percent available is probably worth the associated risks. Mirvis concludes his article with these apropos words given the views I express in this essay: "Who knows where this will take us? Likely as not, to a place we know but have never been before."[63]

Concluding Reflections

In the name of transparency it is important to note that my own spiritual values find their energy in my deeply held Christian convictions. I have had the luxury of teaching in a Christian university where there is no divide between religious commitment and spiritual values. In fact, the language of faith and learning integration is central to the environment where I taught

---

61. Ibid.
62. Ashmos and Duchon, "Spirituality at Work," 135.
63. Mirvis, *"Soul-work in Organizations,"* 204.

for so many years. It is accurate to say that the integration of faith and learning is in the DNA of Northwest Christian University.

These matters are important in light of the ongoing struggle to employ the language of spirituality in workplaces that are not distinctly religious. In fact, the organizations where most of my students will ultimately be employed after graduation will not primarily be religious in nature. They will have to learn for themselves how to "thread the needle" of bringing spirituality into their respective workplaces as they seek meaningful employment after their NCU experience. It is worth observing that while there is no necessary connection between organized religion and spirituality, we cannot ignore the fact that for many people (perhaps most), their core spirituality is expressed with reference to a recognized faith tradition. Such a claim cannot be excluded from our thinking about workplace spirituality.

Bibliography

Alderson, W. T., and N. A. McDonnell. *Theory R Management*. Nashville: Nelson, 1994.

Allchin, A. H., and E. DeWaal. *Daily Readings and Prayers and Praises from the Celtic Tradition*. Springfield, IL: Templegate, 1986.

Ashmos, D. P., and D. Duchon. "Spiritualty at Work: a Conceptualization and Measure." *Journal of Management Inquiry* 9 (2000) 134–45.

Barker, J. A. *Paradigms: The Business of Discovering the Future*. New York: HarperCollins, 1992.

Bartlett, A. B., and S. Goshal. "Changing the Role of Top Management: Beyond Strategy to Purpose." *Harvard Business Review* 72 (1994) 79–88.

Blanchard, K. et al. *Leadership by the Book: Tools to Transform Your Workplace*. New York: Morrow, 1999.

Braham, J. "The Spiritual Side." *Industry Week* 248/3 (1999) 48–56.

Carmichael, A. *Celtic Invocations*. Noroton, CT: Vineyard, 1972.

Chittister, J. *The Rule of Benedict: Insight for the Ages*. New York: Crossroad, 1992.

Cohen, A. "The Guiding Light." *Sales and Management* 149/8 (1997) 46–54.

Conger, J. A. *Spirit at Work: Discovering the Spirituality in Leadership*. San Francisco: Jossey-Bass, 1994.

Conlin, M. "Religion in the Workplace." *Business Week* November 1 (1999) 150–58.

Daft, R. L. *Management*. Fort Worth: Dryden, 2000.

Depree, M. *Leadership is an Art*. New York: Dell, 1989.

———. *Leadership Jazz*. New York: Dell, 1992.

———. *Leading without Power: Finding Hope in Serving Community*. San Francisco: Jossey-Bass, 1997.

DeWaal, E. *God under My Roof: Celtic Songs and Blessings*. Orleans, MA: Paraclete, 1984a.

———. *The Celtic Way of Prayer: The Rediscovery of the Religious Imagination*. New York: Doubleday, 1997.

Elkins, D. N. et al. "Toward a Humanistic-Phenomenological Spirituality: Definition, Description, and measurement." *Journal of Humanistic Psychology* 28/4 (1988) 5–18.

Fayol, H. *General and Industrial Management.* Translated by C. Storrs 1949. London: Pitman & Sons, 1916.
Ferris, T. *The Whole Shebang: A State of the Universe(s) Report.* New York: Simon & Schuster, 1997.
Frick, D. M. and L. C. Spears, eds. *The Private Writings of Robert K. Greenleaf: On Becoming a Servant Leader.* San Francisco: Jossey-Bass, 1996.
Graham, P., ed. *Mary Parker-Follett: Prophet of Management.* Boston: Harvard Business School, 1995.
Greenleaf, R. K. *Servant Leadership.* New York: Paulist, 1977.
———. *Spirituality as Leadership.* Indianapolis: Robert K. Greenleaf Center for Servant-Leadership, 1988.
Handy, C. *The Age of Paradox.* Boston: Harvard Business School, 1994.
Hersey, P., et.al. *Management of Organizational Behavior.* Upper Saddle River, NJ: Prentice Hall, 1996.
Herzberg, F., B. Mausner, and B. B. Snyderman. *The Motivation to Work.* New Brunswick, NJ: Wiley & Sons, 1959.
Herzberg, F. et al. *Job Attitudes: Research and Opinion.* Pittsburgh: Psychological Service of Pittsburgh, 1957.
Jacobsen, S. E. "Spirituality and Transformational Leadership in Secular Settings: A Delphi Study." Ph.D diss., Seattle University, 1994.
Jones, G.R., and J. M. Hill C. W. L. *Contemporary Management.* Boston: Irwin/McGraw Hill, 1998.
Kanigel, R. *The One Best Way: Winslow Taylor and the Enigma of Efficiency.* New York: Penguin, 1997.
Kantrowitz, B. et al. "In Search of the Sacred." *Newsweek* 124/22 (1994) 52–62.
Kennedy, M. H. "Fayol's Principles and the Rule of St. Benedict: Is There Anything New under the Sun?" *Journal of Management History* 5(5) (1999) 269–76.
Kuhn, T. S. *The Structure of Scientific Revolutions.* Chicago: University of Chicago, 1962.
Lee, C., and R. Zemke. "The Search for Spirit in the Workplace." *Training* 30(6) (1993) 21–28.
Maslow, A. H. *Motivation and Personality.* New York: Harper, 1954.
———. *Religions, Values, and Peak-Experiences.* New York: Penguin, 1970.
McGregor, D. *Professional Manager.* New York: McGraw-Hill, 1967.
Mirvis, P. H. "Soul-work in Organizations." *Organization Science* 8(2) (1997) 193–206.
Mitroff, I. I., and E. A. Denton. *A Spiritual Audit of Corporate America.* San Francisco: Jossey-Bass, 1999b.
Moorhouse, G. *Sun Dancing: A Vision of Medieval Ireland.* New York: Harcourt Brace, 1997.
Neal, J. A. "Spirituality in Management: A Guide to Resources." *Journal of Management Education* 21 (1997) 121–39.
Nichols, M. "Does New Age Business Have a Message for Managers?" *Harvard Business Review* 72 (1994) 52–60.
Novak. M. *The Catholic Ethic and the Spirit of Capitalism.* New York: Simon & Schuster, 1993.
———. *Business as a Calling: Work and the Examined Life.* New York: Simon & Schuster, 1996.
Ray, M. L. "Introduction." In *The New Paradigm in Business,* edited by M. L. Ray and A. Rinzler. New York: Penguin, 1993.

Renesch, J., and B. Defoore, eds. *The New Bottom Line*. Pleasonton, CA: New Leaders, 1998.
Senge, P. P. *The Fifth Discipline*. New York: Doubleday, 1990.
Senge, P. P. et al. *The Fifth Discipline Fieldbook*. New York: Doubleday, 1994.
Smith, A. *Power of the Mind*. New York: Ballantine, 1975.
Tawney, R. H. *Religion and the Rise of Capitalism*. Holland Memorial Lectures 1922. 1926. Reprinted, New York: Penguin, 1984.
Taylor, F. W. *The Principles of Scientific Management*. New York: Norton, 1911/1967.
Vaill, P. B. *Managing as a Performing Art*. San Francisco: Jossey-Bass, 1989.
———. *Rediscovering the Soul of Business: A Renaissance of Values*. San Francisco: Sterling & Stone, 1995.
———. *Spirited Leading and Learning*. San Francisco: Jossey-Bass, 1998.
Weber, M. *The Protestant Ethic and the Spirit of Capitalism*. New York: Scribner, 1958.
Wheatley, M. J. *Leadership and the New Science*. San Francisco: Berrett-Koehler, 1992.
Williams, O. F., and J. Houck, eds. *The Judeo-Christian Vision and the Modern Corporation*. Notre Dame, IN: University of Notre Dame Press, 1982.
Wren, D. A. *The Evolution of Management Thought*. New York: Wiley & Sons, 1994.

3

Biblical Preaching and Rhetorical Criticism

George Knox

A Sermon: The Essential Element

WHAT DOES EVERY SERMON need in order to be both Christian and effective? A biblical text? Certainly that would help. But how much text is enough? Content-centered preachers often like to use big chunks of biblical material and yet a sermon may be "biblical" with a short text, or even no formal text at all. Most would say that a sermon must be relevant; that is, it must meet the needs of people. For the psychologically bent proclaimer, the demand for relevance may result in a one-sided approach in which preaching is simply personal counseling on a group scale.

A homiletician with a strong rhetorical bias might insist that every sermon be carefully organized, with introduction, body, and conclusion each performing its proper rhetorical function. Solid structure and scintillating style would be his or her standard for a sermon. The preacher with an institutional orientation will stress the social function of the church as "family," or "body," and run the risk of being a promoter of church functions rather than a proclaimer of the gospel. Theology, social issues, biblical exposition, personal relevance, structure and style, communication techniques, institutional concerns, and many other elements, singly and in combination are important to sermons.

But is there some essential element, without which a sermon would be neither Christian nor effective? Dietrich Bonhoeffer thought there was. On June 24, 1939, while visiting in the United States, he wrote in his diary: "Tomorrow is Sunday. I wonder if I shall hear a sermon."[1] For Bonhoeffer the sermon was one of the forms in which Christ is present *pro me* (for me). The fact of Christ's presence is not in question. The question is really about the kind of structure the manifestation of his person takes which enables me to relate to the person of Christ. Just as the Word came "in the likeness of sinful flesh" and so experienced humiliation, now the Word comes in the words of human messengers. The idea of God, His Word, is found in the address of human beings to each other. Christ is the idea of God, His Word, which becomes *pro me* in the form of an address.[2] It is as Jesus himself said when he commissioned the seventy to help proclaim the good news of the kingdom: "The one who listens to you listens to me, and the one who rejects you rejects me . . ." (Luke 10:16). The foundational assumption in this essay is that in some, admittedly mysterious, way the sermon must communicate Christ or it is not a sermon.

In preaching there is revelation, not of intellectual content, although content is vital, but of Presence, of the sometimes surprising, always mysterious, out-of-our-control Presence of God in Jesus Christ. We call it preaching the Word of God. What preacher, fresh from the pulpit, depressed by a strong feeling that his or her words fell dead about half way from the pulpit to the first row, has not heard the surprising but obviously sincere comment from a parishioner, "what you said today was exactly what I needed." That person, at least, received the Word of God. Christ was present in that message.

Is there anything the preacher can do which will guarantee that this Sunday's sermon will, in fact, communicate the Presence of Christ? Not really. No technique, lowering of lights, mood music, tone of voice, tear jerking story, or sophisticated reasoning, can manipulate the Spirit or force the Presence. Only God, not flesh and blood, can reveal His Word. Nor is there any method by which we can present the Gospel so that its acceptance is guaranteed. Paul Tillich stressed this fact when he said, "To communicate the Gospel means putting it before the people so that they are able to

1. Bonhoeffer, *Christ the Center*, 47–48.
2. Ibid., 50.

decide for or against it . . . All that we who communicate this Gospel can do is to make possible the genuine decision."[3] It is possible for them to hear the Gospel and reject it, but it is also possible for them to never hear the Gospel at all because of my presentation of it. While we cannot develop techniques which guarantee a favorable hearing of the Gospel, we can remove as many human obstacles as possible so that the Gospel can receive a fair hearing. If the "idea of God," Jesus Christ, is hidden in the humiliation of human address, the sound and sense of that address must not be so filled with disconcerting noises or inconsistencies that listeners cannot hear the Word.

The question we began with now becomes "how may I present the sermon so that the communication of Christ is possible?" If "preaching the Word of God" means the communication of the presence of God in Christ, we are talking about the revelation or communication of personality. But what is needed, in preaching, to experience that personality? Psychologists tells us that personality can be defined as "the total pattern of characteristic ways of thinking, feeling, and behaving that constitute the individual's distinctive method of relating to his environment."[4] We come to know a person as we experience the total pattern of that person's characteristic ways of thinking, feeling and acting. As persons created in the image of God we come to know God personally when we experience the way He thinks, feels and acts. There is, consequently, a trinity of needs for every sermon if it is to communicate the Presence of the Holy. This trinity, while considered separately, is so interrelated that any sermon which has but one, or even two, while neglecting the third will be out of balance and distorted.

To convey personality the sermon must have, for one thing, a rational character. It must make sense. Through ideas, concepts, logical argumentation, information, and all kinds of rational discourse it will demonstrate a way of thinking. It must be intellectually honest, creative and challenging. For "biblical" preaching this requires faithfulness to the ideas, the logic and the argument of the text. It means taking seriously the content of the scriptures. Ronald Allen raises a serious question at this point by saying that biblical illiteracy is no longer unusual among main-line clergy. By biblical illiteracy he means "a lack of familiarity with the content of the scriptures as well as uncertainty about how to interpret them. . . . On one level, many of us do not know basic facts of the biblical stories . . . On another level, we are not always sure of the meaning of biblical texts or what, if anything,

---

3. Tillich, *Theology of Culture*, 201.
4. Kegan and Havermann, *Psychology: an Introduction*, 401.

they have to do with us."⁵ If preachers cannot handle the intellectual and factual content of the Bible they run the risk of placing huge stumbling blocks between their listeners and the Gospel.

But the person of Christ is not known through rational content in a sermon alone any more than we know other people only through the impact of their thinking. Ideas and arguments are inseparably linked with feelings, dreams and hopes. Unless the ideas are charged by and expressed with all of the ethos and feelings found in persons, the sermon will fall back dead. Nor will a sermon convey the person of Christ without serious stumbling blocks if the second leg of the triangle, the communication of feeling, is missing.

For "biblical" preaching to communicate feelings the preacher needs to consider what feelings are expressed by the author in the text, how they are expressed, how the author's words might have affected the first readers in their situation, and how this text makes its present readers feel. The sermon thus tries to express the personal feelings in the text by taking its emotional material, often expressed in the form of ancient metaphors and imagery, including stories, and reusing it in new and creative ways. The story of the text can then merge with the stories of the preacher and audience.

The third element needed to communicate Presence is a sense of purpose. Because we have wills and are capable of choosing one direction over another we sense the need for purpose direction, and a goal in life. To be sure, this goal-oriented character of our personalities can lead to neurotic, rigid, and compulsory actions. But such distortions only speak to the need we have for direction rather than aimlessness, for purpose and specific objectives rather than vague uncertainties.

Many sermons fail precisely at this point. They may have good intellectual content, including sound biblical exposition; and they may express their ideas with power through the use of story or metaphor, but they don't go anywhere. Such sermons are, as Haddon Robinson put it, "like a dropped lemon meringue pie—they splatter over everything but hit nothing very hard!"⁶ When a sermon has no clear objective the listener may find it interesting or even enjoyable, but have a nagging question in his or her mind: "What do I do now? What was the point of it all?" Or, more bluntly, "So what?"

---

5. Allen, *Contemporary Biblical Interpretation for Preaching*, 15–16.
6. Robinson, Biblical Preaching, 107.

Biblical Preaching and Rhetorical Criticism

Seeking a purpose makes one ask, "Why am I preaching this sermon?" But the preacher of biblical sermons will ask first some performative questions such as, "What is the purpose of this text?" and "What is the language of the text doing?" These questions may then translate into the craftsman's query, "What must my sermon seek to do?"[7] These questions will help the preacher develop a truly biblical sermon.

In order to discover the purpose of a passage a careful analysis of the life-situation must be made. What is the occasion which called forth this particular text? What alterations in his audience's attitude, behavior, or values is the author seeking to achieve? A definition of the problem being addressed, the attitudinal or behavioral changes sought, and a description of how the author goes about trying to influence the readers, are all necessary to establish purpose.

A rhetorical analysis of the text will help the preacher establish his persuasive purpose. Aristotle's definition of rhetoric as "the faculty of discovering in the particular case all the available means of persuasion"[8] points to a rhetorical analysis which looks at a text in order to discover the author's persuasive purpose and the means by which he or she seeks to achieve it. This in turn lays the groundwork for asking "What is the objective of this sermon?"

A rhetorical methodology is appropriate biblical study in preparation for preaching because the biblical text itself is rhetorical in nature, that is, each book or letter was written to particular people for the purpose of altering behavior, beliefs, and/or attitudes. The authors did not take up pen to simply jot down a few pleasantries or to demonstrate their skill at writing pleasing sentences. They had a persuasive purpose in mind and made use of arguments, metaphors, figures, word pictures—all kinds of rhetorical devices to accomplish their purposes. Furthermore, these authors, while they may not have had formal training in rhetoric, lived and wrote in an environment where rhetoric was the universal subject of education. "Palestine and Syria were not rhetorical backwaters," claims George A. Kennedy, who cites specific evidence to indicate that authors of New Testament books if not trained in rhetoric, at least had rhetorical skills and wrote to people who were familiar with rhetorical practices.[9]

---

7. Buttrick, "Interpretation and Preaching," 58.
8. Aristotle, *The Rhetoric of Aristotle*, 7.
9. Kennedy, *New Testament Interpretation through Rhetorical Criticism*, 9

Paul's Letters Rhetorical in Nature

Paul's letters are particularly suited to this approach because of their explicit argumentative nature. In the midst of a letter characterized by argumentation and emotional appeal he wrote: "knowing, therefore, the fear of the Lord, we persuade people" (2 Cor 5:11). As a preacher of the gospel and the author of letters to churches with problems, it was necessary for Paul to engage in persuasion, which is understood here as the inducement of the willing modification of beliefs, attitudes, values, or behavior by means of discourse. The modification may range along a continuum from strengthening resistance to change on one end of the continuum to actually bringing about change on the other. Paul's attempts at persuasion found him working all along this continuum, addressing a vigorous rhetoric to a variety of circumstances. Divisions in the church, cases of immorality, questions about the resurrection and the second coming and problems pertaining to worship, were just a few situations which he addressed.

Did he address them not with rhetorical language but with "sacred language," which is the straightforward use of an authoritative proclamation, a "thus saith the Lord," without argumentation?[10] Such authoritative proclamations of doctrine without accompanying reasons can be found in the Bible. Jesus, for example, ordinarily did not argue for his message on the basis of probability; he simply proclaimed it. Paul, on the other hand often used enthymenes which, simply defined, are assertions with supporting reasons. In Rom 1:18–19 for example: "The wrath of God is revealed ... because ..." The use of "because" or "for" with a statement usually introduces the supporting reason, a typical feature of Paul's rhetoric. Occasionally, Paul may give an authoritative word from the Lord, as in 1 Cor 7:10, "But to the married I give instructions, not I, but the Lord, that the wife should not leave her husband." But even here he adds an explanatory parenthesis which softens the instructions somewhat ("but if she does leave, let her remain unmarried ...")

Several analyses of Paul's letters have demonstrated their rhetorical nature. He tries to persuade a Christian slave owner, Philemon, to receive back a runaway slave who has become a Christian. The rhetorical design of this letter indicates that Paul was a master of rhetorical persuasion, whether trained or not.[11] One may disagree with Hans Dieter Betz regarding the

---

10. Ibid., 6–7.
11. Betz, *Galatians*.

details of the rhetorical structure of Gal, but his commentary has made a strong case for the "apologetic" and rhetorical nature of the letter.[12] At the very least Paul was attempting to strengthen the adherence of the Galatians to beliefs he had implanted.

Wilhelm Wuellner, in a study of Romans, has proposed that Paul's letters be considered on the basis of argumentation rather than on the basis of modern theories of literature (Wuellner March 1976).[13] On more than one occasion, all of the persuasive powers at Paul's command were brought to bear upon the situation at Corinth in order to alter, and even reverse some of their ideas and actions. George Kennedy has identified 2 Cor as judicial rhetoric, one of the three species of rhetorical speech described by Aristotle. Judicial rhetoric calls upon the audience to make a judgment about past events. First Corinthians on the other hand, is largely deliberative, a type of rhetorical speech which seeks to persuade the listeners to take some action in the future although it contains some judicial passages.[14] It appears reasonable, therefore, to say that a knowledge of rhetorical principles and their application to the study of Pauline literature could be helpful to the biblical scholar and preacher.

Because rhetoric enjoyed a central place in all Hellenistic education at that time discourse and persuasion were inseparably linked in the Hellenistic mind. Did Paul object to the importance of rhetoric and reject all attempts at persuasion when he wrote in 1 Cor 2:11ff that he did not come to them with "superiority of speech" or "persuasive words of wisdom?" Is he involved in a contradiction, practicing persuasion while pretending to reject it? This problem can be resolved by remembering one of the major historical developments in rhetorical theory and practice, the emphasis upon declamations which had become popular by Paul's time. Aristotle's definition and treatment of rhetoric had placed the emphasis more upon proof than style, while other rhetoricians in subsequent years began to focus more upon style. Quintilian, the most famous rhetorician of the first century AD, called rhetoric "the knowledge of how to speak well" and featured in his textbook a variety of rhetorical devices which do not neglect proof but give increased attention to style.[15]

---

12. Ibid.
13. Wuellner, "Paul's Rhetoric of Argumentation in Romans."
14. Kennedy, *New Testament Interpretation through Rhetorical Criticism*, chap. 5.
15. Ibid.

Most likely, it is the inordinate emphasis upon style which Paul rejects in 1 Cor 2. By his time declamations had become a popular means of entertainment. But declaimers often neglected argumentation and for proof relied upon the appeal of their personality, emotion, and general hyperbole.[16] Many declaimers were interested in immediate personal effectiveness while Aristotle, Cicero, Tacitus, Quintilian and other leading rhetoricians of the classical period believed rhetoric should energize knowledge and humanize truth.[17] Paul's rejection of "persuasive words" in 1 Corinthians 2 and his admission in 2 Corinthians 10:6 that he was "unskilled in speech," while insisting that he was not inferior in knowledge, indicates only that his style and motivation were different from that of the declaimers. He wants people to understand that the purpose of his speech was not to make a personal impression but to convince others of the truth.

Was Paul trained in rhetoric? Because rhetorical schools were common in the Hellenized cities of the east when Paul was a boy, it is possible that he attended one. In Paul's day speech was considered to be the greatest human art, a view which led Tacitus, a contemporary of Paul, to be appalled at the inadequacy of Nero who was unable to compose his own speeches.[18] Someone as well educated as Paul could hardly miss receiving at least some training in rhetoric. Nor was it uncommon for Jews to receive such training.[19] Paul may or may not have had formal training in rhetoric. It is clear, however, that he lived in a world which for several centuries had been exposed to rhetorical education. It is appropriate, therefore, to try to hear his words as a Greek-speaking audience would have heard them.

Paul as Preacher

Another reason for adopting a rhetorical perspective when studying Paul's epistles is that he is more preacher than writer and theologian. His style and structure carry the typical marks of a preacher and rhetorician. He wrote the way he spoke, a practice recommended by Quintilian for orators (Scroggs 1976). Since he often used a secretary his words were written, presumably, while he spoke, giving them the sense of speech. He expected his letters to be read aloud in the church (Col 4:16). He speaks directly to his

---

16. Ibid.
17. Baldwin, *Ancient Rhetoric and Poetic*, 247
18. Kennedy, *New Testament Interpretation through Rhetorical Criticism*, 512.
19. Ibid., 9.

readers, with a dramatic immediacy using imaginary dialogue, accusations and defenses as though he were in court, questions and exclamations.[20] Recognizing such features led Leander Keck to predict that scholars would make more use of rhetorical analysis for interpreting Paul. "In the long run," he stated, "comparing Paul's letters with ancient rhetoric may be more important than comparing them with ancient letters.[21]

Rhetorical Theory

The strategies used here to analyze Pauline texts for the purpose of preaching grow out of the rhetorical theory developed by such men of the classical and New Testament periods as Plato, Aristotle, Cicero, and Quintilian. Aristotle, who expanded upon Plato's treatment of rhetoric in the *Phaedrus* and in *Gorgias*, provided the foundation for rhetorical theory in his work *Rhetoric*, not by inventing rhetoric but by describing what he observed. He assumed that discourse followed universal rhetorical patterns. His definition of rhetoric, his descriptions of proofs, and his identification of the critical roles played by speaker, listener, and speech in the rhetorical situation, still provide a standard for modern rhetoricians. During the Roman period, which takes us into the time of Paul, there were many outstanding rhetoricians, of whom Cicero and Quintilian are the best known. Quintilian is of particular interest because he lived during the first century A.D. and was the author of the largest Latin rhetorical treatise which survives from antiquity, *Education of the Orator*. His work reflects the importance rhetoric held for education in the first century.

Species of Rhetoric

Some critics have said Aristotle was not familiar with all forms of rhetoric. Specifically they point to what is called "cultic" or "sacred" rhetoric,[22] a kind used in synagogue and church as well as in the Bible which often has an authoritative, "thus saith the Lord," character. This declarative kind of language is difficult to classify under one of Aristotle's three species of speeches, forensic, epideictic, or deliberative, and may be considered as a

---

20. Wildner, *Early Christian Rhetoric*, 15
21. Keck, *Paul and His Letters*, 1979.
22. Olbricht, "Rhetorical Criticism of the New Testament," 4.

fourth species for the purposes of biblical study. Nevertheless, the rhetorical critic will be aided by knowing the primary characteristics of each species identified by Aristotle, while keeping in mind that not all biblical speech will fall under one of them.

The forensic species of rhetoric was traditionally associated with the court room and was used in accusation and defense.[23] Forensic speech occurs when the speaker recognizes something about a situation which in his or her opinion needs to be corrected. Something has happened, a person has acted or spoken in some unacceptable manner, or some wrong has occurred. Forensic speech is used then to persuade an audience to make judgments about such past events. Enthymemes, logical arguments in the form of a premise accompanied by a conclusion, Aristotle said, are best suited for this type of rhetoric because they address three situations: (1) the cause and varieties of wrong doing, (2) the states of mind in which people do wrong, and (3) the persons likely to be wronged.[24] Second Corinthians, for example, because it argues for the authenticity of Paul's past as well as present ministry and against the position of his opponents is an example of forensic discourse.

Epideictic speech aims at persuading an audience to hold or reaffirm some point of view in the present. It offers praise or blame and is concerned with virtue and vice, the noble and the base in order to strengthen adherence to a particular position or to persuade the audience to modify its opinion.[25] The method best suited to this endeavor is magnification or expanding upon the thesis and thus emphasizing the good or the bad. Typically, epideictic speech in the classical period was characteristic of funeral orations and cultic activities. Paul often used this kind of speech in his letters in order to reaffirm through amplification the essential message which they had heard from him in the beginning.

Exhortation, encouragement and dissuasion characterize deliberative speech.[26] It seeks to persuade the listener either to adopt or reject an action, "for the one who exhorts recommends a course of action as better and the one who dissuades deters us from it as worse."[27] Deliberative speech, then, offers advice, attempting to move people to take some action in the future.

23. Aristotle, The *Rhetoric of Aristotle*, 17.
24. Ibid., 54–67.
25. Ibid., 54.
26. Ibid., 17.
27. Ibid., 18

Aristotle observed its use primarily in the councils of government. Again, all of Paul's letters contain elements of deliberative speech as Paul urged his readers to act in certain ways. Keeping in mind these three species will help identify the purposes of Paul.

Persuasive Proofs

By definition the goal of rhetoric is persuasion. It reaches this goal through the interaction of speaker (writer), speech (text), and listener (reader). Since persuasion is its goal, rhetoric does not deal with certainty, or demonstrative proof, but with probabilities. It is thus concerned with proofs which persuade. Such proof is either invented for the occasion or already existent, "artistic" or "non-artistic," Aristotle tells us.[28] The non-artistic are external documents or witnesses not found in the speech itself. The artistic means of persuasion are three in type and are invented by the speaker. They encompass the three elements of a rhetorical situation: the speaker the listener and the speech itself.

The proof inherent in the speaker, labeled *ethos* by Aristotle, leads to persuasion when the speech is so uttered as to make the speaker worthy of belief.[29] He goes on to say that credibility is established when the audience, through the speaker's work, gains the perception that he or she is intelligent, of virtuous character, and has good will.[30]

The second kind of proof is *pathos* which is inherent in the audience and may be defined as "the emotional reactions the hearers undergo as the orator plays upon their feelings."[31] The appeal to emotion is designed to result in the "good will" and "friendly disposition" of a listener and thus put him or her in a frame of mind to respond favorably to the argument.[32] Cicero was of the opinion that the decisions people make are based more on feelings than on facts. His observation has proven accurate. The speaker must, therefore, have a clear idea of what people are feeling, as well as thinking in order to rebut feeling with feeling.[33] Rhetorical choices of emotional as well as logical arguments will be shaped by the attitudes found within the

28. Ibid., 8.
29. Ibid.
30. Ibid., 92.
31. Kennedy, *New Testament Interpretation through Rhetorical Critcism*, 15.
32. Aristotle, The *Rhetoric of Aristotle*, 92.
33. Baldwin, *Ancient Rhetoric and Poetic*, 52.

audience. Consequently, audience analysis is a preliminary concern of the speaker before engaging in the process of message construction.

Likewise, audience analysis is a vital preliminary step for the interpretation of a written discourse. A certain amount of knowledge about the audience can be derived from background studies of a historical, sociological, and cultural nature. Other vital information can be gained by looking at the text itself to discover adaptation strategies which reveal the nature of the rhetorical audience as perceived by the author. For example, the Greek concept of excellence is apparently important to the audience that Paul addressed in Phil. Personified in the goddess *Arete*, the Greek idea of excellence provided an emotional and intellectual base upon which Paul built his argument in chapter three reaching its climax in 3:13–16 with the image of striving upward to the goal in Christ.

The third type of persuasive proof is inherent in the speech itself. Aristotle called it *logos*, by which he meant logical argumentation. As he put it: "Persuasion is effected by the arguments, when we demonstrate the truth, real or apparent by such means as inhere in particular cases."[34] Two modes of reasoning are available to the speaker, induction and deduction. Inductive reasoning takes the form of the example; the deductive mode takes the form of the enthymeme. Both are based upon probability. For scientific certainty induction would have to employ complete or extended enumeration of examples. A speaker, because of limitations of time, attention and interest span of the audience, cannot give complete enumeration of instances. The speaker, therefore, offers a few cogent examples to support his or her argument.

Similarly, syllogisms are used to establish certainty in deductive reasoning. Speakers however, do not generally speak in syllogistic patterns. Rather, they employ the enthymeme. A syllogism contains three parts: the major premise, the minor premise, and the conclusion. Generally, in the enthymeme two of the parts are combined and one is dropped. The essential difference between them is that "the syllogism leads to a necessary conclusion from universally true premises but the enthymeme leads to a tentative conclusion from probable premises."[35] For example, the statement, "John will fail his exam because he has not studied," is an enthymeme. The minor premise is true: John has not studied. The major premise is not universally

---

34. Aristotle, The *Rhetoric of Aristotle*, 9.
35. Corbett, *Classical Rhetoric for the Modern Student*, 73.

true: anyone who has not studied will fail. But it is probable, and therefore persuasive.

Enthymemes can be recognized by their common syntactic pattern and the unlimited number of function words which they employ. Usually they take the form of a compound sentence, the two clauses joined by such conjunctions as "for," "so," "therefore," "since," "because," and the like.[36] The two clauses in the enthymeme are always propositions or theses. "John Smith would not make a good governor; he has communist leanings," is an enthymeme. "He didn't go to the lecture because he had a headache," is not an enthymeme because the second part is only a reason, not a premise from which a conclusion can be deduced.

Both example and enthymeme are logical forms of reasoning but Aristotle preferred the latter. While he recognized that arguments through the use of examples are highly persuasive, he concluded that "arguments in the form of enthymeme are more applauded."[37]

This concern for logically valid argument also reveals his awareness that *ethos* and *pathos* are too often more influential than *logos* and are the most likely to be used in a manipulative manner. At the same time the ancient rhetoricians recognized that *ethos* and *pathos* are essential to the effective use of logical argument. Cicero for example, converted the three proofs into three duties of the orator: to teach (*logos*), to please (*ethos*), and to move (*pathos*). Later, taking his cue from Cicero, Augustine said that the preacher must please in order to maintain the interest of his or her audience in order to teach them and move them to action.[38] A balanced use of each means of proof will appeal to the whole person, the trinity that composes personality—thinking, feeling and willing. Consequently, the interaction of *ethos, pathos* and *logos* must be examined when studying the argument of the text in order to apply the whole text to the whole person.

The three modes of persuasion are brought to bear through the use of five canons: (1) Invention, the planning of a discourse and its arguments; (2) Arrangement, the organization of the various parts of a discourse into an effective whole; (3) Style, the choice of words, composition of sentences and the use of figures; (4) Memory; and, (5) Delivery. The latter, memory and delivery, will need no further comment since they are not relevant to the study of texts.

---

36. Ibid., 77.
37. Aristotle, *The Rhetoric of Aristotle* 10.
38. Kennedy, *New Testament Interpretation through Rhetorical Criticism*, 18.

Invention

Generally, the procedure for developing a speech or a text moves from the choice of a topic to the definition of a thesis aimed at accomplishing the speaker's rhetorical purpose. Next comes the selection of material most suitable for the particular audience from one's existing knowledge, observation, or from universal categories, what Aristotle called *topoi*. By the use of these topics the speaker amplifies the thesis and develops the basic issue of the speech or text. Rhetorical analysis of a text, therefore includes the identification of the basic issue, the theses and sub-theses pertaining to the issue, and description of how enthymeme, example, and rhetorical figures of thought and speech interact to form persuasive proofs.

Arrangement

The second canon of rhetoric, arrangement, seeks to discover the rhetorically effective composition of the message and mold its elements into a unified structure. Roman rhetoricians expanded upon Aristotle's original description of a speech's essential elements of proposition and argument with a proem and epilogue by identifying five elements of arrangement: (1) Introduction which seeks to gain attention and good will and which often creates anticipation in the listener by hinting at the primary subjects to be discussed; (2) Narration of the facts or background information; (3) Proof, the presentation of the proposition, often with a partition of it into separate headings, and the arguments which support it; (4) Refutation of opposing views; (5) Conclusion which summarizes and seeks to arouse emotions and move the audience to action.[39] The order and strength of arguments within both proof and refutation also need consideration. Cicero's advice was to place the strongest argument first and the weakest in the middle.[40]

The functions and characteristics of these elements of arrangement may serve as guides for discovering the rhetorical units of a text and the contribution each makes to the overall argument. However, one should not think that these elements compose a pattern which New Testament authors followed rigidly. It remains to be seen when studying a Pauline letter whether or not he followed the usual rhetorical pattern of arrangement. Nevertheless it should be helpful to keep in mind the characteristics of each

---

39. Golden, and Goodwin, *The Rhetoric of Western Thought*, 23–24.
40. Sutton, *De Orators*, 435.

of the five elements of arrangement and to test Paul's organization of his letter by them. Furthermore, rhetorical analysis will consider the arrangement of texts as they stand and ask whether or not there is a rhetorical function for apparent literary problems such illogical breaks, interpolations and other problems within the text.

Style

Language presents the speaker and writer with many choices and style is the group of selections that one makes from among the possible choices presented. It has to do with words, phrases, sentences, images, figures, pauses, and rhythm. The function of style is first to enhance understanding and retention by providing clarity, appropriateness, and vividness to speech.[41] Secondly, style shapes perception and influences behavior by the dynamic combination of emotional, rational, and image-creating words and sentences. Style can be gratuitous ornamentation and conceit, but in the best writers, "it is functional and varies with the author's intent. It is one of his persuasive tools."[42]

Rhetorical Analysis for Preaching

Before describing the elements of rhetorical analysis which may be used for the study of Pauline texts a word of caution must be given. The rhetorical theory described here cannot be rigidly applied simply because Paul does not seem to follow any rigid rhetorical patterns. The work of Hans Dieter Betz is criticized for his strict and limited application to Gal of the principles involved in the canon of arrangement. In an earlier age the canon of style was the center of attention and led scholars to focus on word usage, particularly the tropes and figures of classical rhetoric.[43] If any canon offers more possibilities than others for use in biblical study, it is that of invention which emphasizes argumentation and the interaction of the three modes of persuasion. However, a holistic and flexible approach is most adequate. An exclusive use of one canon or another will be atomistic, resulting in a fragmented perception of the text. The key is to see the dynamic relation-

---

41. Aristotle, *The Rhetoric of Aristotle*, 182.
42. Kennedy, *New Testament Interpretation through Rhetorical Criticism*, 25.
43. Olbricht, "Rhetorical Criticism of the New Testament," 4–5.

ship between invention, arrangement, and style, with invention providing the foundational base of the triangle.

How can these basic rhetorical principles be put to use for the analysis of Pauline texts as one prepares to preach? Presumably the preacher who wants results also wants to treat the text with integrity. This requires preaching sermons which fit the rhetorical purpose of the text. A sermon that is not in tune with the intent of the biblical author will not be a truly "biblical" sermon. The first goal of rhetorical analysis, therefore, is to state precisely the rhetorical purpose of the author. Several steps are needed to accomplish this goal. Although these steps are isolated for the sake of discussion it should be recognized that they often overlap or are circular.

First, determine the rhetorical species of the text. Is it forensic, epideictic, or deliberative? And does the text contain a great deal of "sacred" language? Clues to understanding the meaning of each unit in the letter or book are provided by determining the species. As noted earlier, each species has certain characteristics. Deliberative rhetoric has a preponderance of examples and advises specific courses of action. Epideictic speech relies upon devices that magnify and expand upon the good or the bad qualities of a person, institution, or value. It is fond of ornament, description, and makes great use of the imagination and inspiration.[44] Forensic speech relies upon enthymeme and is more thesis oriented. By noticing the rhetorical strategies and devices used by the author the species can be determined which in turn implies something about the author's purpose.

Second, define the rhetorical situation, which corresponds roughly to the *Sitz im Leben* of form criticism. The items considered, however, are rhetorically oriented. Lloyd F. Bitzer has provided a helpful description of the items that need to be considered. Of primary importance is the identity of the rhetorical audience. The usual data bank of social, historical, political, and general demographic information is necessary. Especially important, however, is the identification of the particular rhetorical audience. Bitzer comments, ". . . a rhetorical audience must be distinguished from a body of mere hearers or readers: properly speaking, a rhetorical audience consists only of those persons who are capable of being influenced by discourse and of being mediators of change."[45] The first place to look for indicators of the rhetorical audience is within the text itself. Names, groups of people mentioned, salutations, and descriptions given by the author, such as in 1

---

44. Ibid., 75.
45. Bitzer, "The Rhetorical Situation," 253.

Cor 1:26–28 ("not many wise . . ."), are helpful indicators. Knowing there are opponents of Paul in Corinth and discovering their characteristics is also helpful. Although it is clear that Paul is not addressing his opponents directly, he believes they have influenced his readers and this colors his perception of the audience.

The audience plays a critical role in a speaker or writer's selection of materials and arguments. "It is indeed the audience which has the major role in determining the quality of argument and the behavior of orators."[46] One must look for the kind of audience the author has in mind, therefore, in the types of figures, rhetorical devices, and arguments he or she uses to adapt the speech to the audience. Consequently, a final decision on the particular rhetorical audience cannot be made without studying the argument, which reminds us of the circular nature of these stages of analysis.

Another task required for defining the rhetorical situation is the identification of constraints. This task moves the process one step further while at the same time refines the definition of the rhetorical audience. Bitzer explains constraints as follows:

> Every rhetorical situation contains a set of constraints made up of persons, events, objects and relations which are parts of the situation because they have the power to constrain decision and action needed to modify the exigency. Standard sources of constraint include beliefs, attitudes, documents, facts, traditions, images, interests, motives and the like; and when the orator enters the situation, his discourse not only harnesses constraints given by the situation but provides additional important constraints—for example, his personal character, his logical proofs, and his style.[47]

In many situations the speaker will face one predominant problem which will come to light in the search for constraints. An audience, for example, may be prejudiced against the speaker. For the study of Pauline letters it will be necessary to look for constraints brought to the situation by whatever congregation Paul is addressing, by his opponents, and by Paul himself, and to ask whether or not one overriding problem faces him.

Next, the exigency must be defined. An exigency "is an imperfection marked by urgency; it is a defect, an obstacle, something waiting to be done, a thing which is other than it should be."[48] The interpreter asks,

---

46. Perelman, *The Realm of Rhetoric*, 24.
47. Bitzer, *The Rhetorical Situation*, 254.
48. Ibid., 252.

what is the urgent need which must be met, and can be met by means of discourse? Furthermore, Bitzer adds, "in any rhetorical situation there will be at least one controlling exigency which functions as the organizing principle: it specifies the audience to be addressed and the change to be effected."[49] It is necessary, therefore, to ask of the particular letter or book is there one controlling exigency? If so, what audience is addressed? And what change is sought? Are there several pressing needs or problems? Perhaps the audience shifts. Perhaps the change sought is different in various parts of the book. If there appear to be several exigencies are they related to one, perhaps unexpressed, over-arching need or problem? Or could they represent a series of letters rather than one unified letter?

At this point in the process, after identifying the species and defining the rhetorical situation, the persuasive purpose of the author should be in view. A tentative statement, as concise as possible should be made and tested by the next stage in the process. Only a tentative statement can be made because of the circular nature of the steps; further steps may well lead to revisions.

The third action in rhetorical analysis, in addition to defining the species and the situation, is to analyze the argument. Two major steps are involved in this task which correspond to the classical rhetorical fields of arrangement and invention.

Arrangement includes the traditional divisions of a speech into its various parts. William Brandt supplies two categories for considering the arrangement of a rhetorical work, Structural and Textual rhetoric, which will be used here.[50] Structural rhetoric refers to the parts of the argument and their relation to each other. It deals with the piece as a whole and with the paragraphs as the basic argumentative units. The task is to discover the structural enthymeme, the arguments used to construct it, and their relation to one another.

Structural rhetorical analysis, therefore, includes two actions. First, it seeks to discover whether or not the text contains the traditional parts of a speech: a beginning section which accomplishes the purpose of an Introduction, followed by a Narration, a Proposition, and Proof, and a rhetorical

---

49. Ibid., 253.
50. Brandt, *The Rhetoric of Argumentation*, viii.

Conclusion

These parts move the argument along. It is important to ask how these parts work together or fail to do so toward some unifying purpose in meeting the rhetorical situation. Identifying them also helps to separate rhetorical units. These rhetorical units in turn may serve as texts for expository sermons. Being aware of these units and their relationship to the whole is a valuable hermeneutical step toward preaching sermons which are consistent with the author's intended meaning and purpose.

The second action needed in order to discover the structural argument occurs at the paragraph level and consists in identifying inductive and deductive arguments. The use of specific cases in the form of examples, illustrations, and models, leading to a conclusion reveals the inductive nature of the argument.[51] Often a combination of inductive and deductive arguments can be seen. As the examples, illustrations, and models build toward a conclusion several theses will be implied along the way. These implied assertions will most likely be parts of enthymemes. The task, therefore, is to examine each paragraph, identify the enthymeme or thesis contained therein, note their relationship to one another and arrive at the structural enthymeme or thesis for the work as a whole. This will reveal the unifying theme and its sub-themes within the text. It is also necessary to watch for asides, digressions, emotional outbursts, and the like, and to ask whether or not they accomplish a rhetorical purpose. For example, a digression may serve as a prolepsis, answering questions that are in the mind of the audience before the basic theme can be developed.

First Cor 1–4 provides a good example of a complete rhetorical unit that contains the traditional parts of a speech. The Introduction can be seen in 1:1–9. While Paul utilizes the form of a letter he also uses the opening as an introduction by anticipating some of the critical topics he will deal with later. The Proposition follows in 1:10 and asserts the need for the Corinthians to be united. A Narration follows in 1:11–17 in which Paul refers to the quarrels and divisions among them. The Proof is then presented in the form of an argument that continues to the end of the unit where Paul's rhetorical conclusion can be seen in 4:14–21. The Proof presented in the argument from 1:18 through 4:13 can be seen by looking at each paragraph and arriving at a thesis that summarizes the point being made. Once this is done for each paragraph an outline can be made that organizes the argument into main and sub points.

---

51. Kennedy, *New Testament Interpretation through Rhetorical Criticism*, 99.

Textual rhetorical analysis calls for identifying the rhetorical devices at the paragraph, sentence, and word levels which support the argument. It considers style, the ways words and sentences are manipulated by the author to produce figures of speech and logical devices which clarify, amplify, or in other ways provide persuasive support for enthymemes.[52] Of particular importance in the textual rhetoric is the persuasive role played by metaphorical language.

So far the emphasis here has been placed upon discovering the logical argumentation, what Aristotle called *logos*. It must not be forgotten that *logos* is never really separated from *ethos* or p*athos*. George Kennedy points out that even in Greek oratory, and almost always in religious discourse, logical arguments are introduced only to support details of *ethos* or *pathos*. He comments: "Matthew and Paul make extensive use of the forms of logical argument, but the validity of their arguments is entirely dependent on their assumptions, which cannot be logically and objectively proved."[53] It is necessary, therefore, to be sensitive to Paul's appeals which, while using enthymeme, or logical argument, rely largely upon ethical and emotional factors.

The rhetorical nature of Paul's letters makes the use of rhetorical analysis an appropriate tool for textual interpretation. It, of necessity, calls into use other disciplines such as historical and literary criticism, but it also provides a perspective which is helpful to the preacher as it seeks the rhetorical purpose of the letter and of particular preaching passages. This methodology, also organizes other interpretive disciplines into definable steps and at the same time shows the relationship of their results to each other. For instance, as one moves from the identification of rhetorical species to a description of the rhetorical situation, to argument analysis, the relationship between *Sitz im Leben* and argument begins to stand out. Also, the relationship between individual periscopes and rhetorical units can be seen because the methodology contributes to a holistic concept of the text. This should help the preacher keep from treating a particular passage out of context.

Finally, as the preacher proceeds through the various stages of analysis he or she will at the same time naturally be thinking of how the situation of the letter may parallel his or her own particular audience and of how the whole text applied to the whole person will, prayerfully, make it possible that the Word of God, Christ Himself, may be known.

---

52. Perelman, *The Realm of Rhetoric*, 106.
53. Kennedy, *New Testament Interpretation through Rhetorical Criticism*, 17

Biblical Preaching and Rhetorical Criticism

Bibliography

Allen, Ronald J. *Contemporary Biblical Interpretation for Preaching.* Valley Forge, PA: Judson, 1984.
Aristotle. *The Rhetoric of Aristotle.* An Expanded Translation by Lane Cooper. New York: Appleton-Century-Crofts, 1932.
Baldwin, Charles Sears. *Ancient Rhetoric and Poetic.* Gloucester, MA: Peter Smith, 1959.
Betz, Hans Dieter. *Galatians: A Commentary on Paul's Letter to the Churches in Galatia.* Hermeneia. Philadelphia: Fortress, 1979.
Bitzer, Lloyd D. "The Rhetorical Situation." *Philosophy of Rhetoric* 1 (1968) 1-14.
Bonhoeffer, Dietrich. *Christ the Center.* Introduced by Edwin H. Robertson and translated by John Bowden. San Francisco: Harper & Row, 1960.
Brandt, William J. *The Rhetoric of Argumentation.* Indianapolis: Dobbs-Merrill, 1970.
Buttrick, David. "Interpretation and Preaching." *Interpretation* 35 (1981) 46-58.
Church, F. Forrester. "Rhetorical Structure and Design in Paul's Letter to Philemon." *Harvard Theological Review* 71 (1978) 17-33.
Cicero. *De Orators.* Vol. I. Translated by E.W. Sutton. Cambridge: Harvard University Press, 1959.
Corbett, Edward P. J. *Classical Rhetoric for the Modern Student.* New York: Oxford University Press, 1971.
Golden, James L., Goodwin F. Berquist, and William E. Coleman. *The Rhetoric of Western Thought.* Dubuque, IA: Kendall/Hunt, 1976.
Keck, Leander E. *Paul and His Letters.* Proclamation Commentaries. Philadelphia: Fortress, 1979.
Kegan, Jerome, and Ernst Havemann. *Psychology: An Introduction.* New York: Harcourt Brace Jovanovich, 1972.
Kennedy, George A. *New Testament Interpretation through Rhetorical Criticism.* Chapel Hill: University of North Carolina Press, 1984.
Olbricht, Thomas H. "Rhetorical Criticism of the New Testament: Betz on Galatians." Mimeographed ms. Abilene: Abilene Christian University, n.d.
Perelman, Chaim. *The Realm of Rhetoric.* Translated by William Kluback. Notre Dame: Notre Dame Press, 1982.
Perelman, Chaim, and L. Olbrechts-Tyteca. *The New Rhetoric: A Treatise on Argumentation.* Translated by John Wilkinson and Purcell Weaver. Notre Dame: Notre Dame University Press, 1969.
Robinson, Haddon. *Biblical Preaching.* Grand Rapids: Baker, 1980.
Scroggs, Robin. "Paul as Rhetorician: Two Homilies in Romans 1-11." In *Jews, Greeks and Christians: Religious Cultures in Late Antiquity: Essays in Honor of William David Davies,* edited by Robert Hamerton-Kelly and Robin Scroggs, 271-98. Studies in Judaism in Late Antiquity 21. Leiden: Brill, 1976.
Tillich, Paul. *Theology of Culture.* New York: Oxsford University Press, 1959.
Wilder, Amos N. *Early Christian Rhetoric: The Language of the Gospel.* Cambridge: Harvard University Press, 1964.
Wuellner, Wilhelm. "Paul's Rhetoric of Argumentation in Romans." *Catholic Biblical Quarterly* 38 (1976) 330-51.

4

The Scribe Who Has Been Trained for the Kingdom

A Biblical Theological Perspective on Faith and Learning

Dennis R. Lindsay

> "Therefore every scribe who has been trained for the kingdom of heaven is like the master of a household who brings out of his treasure what is new and what is old."
>
> —Matt 13:52 (NRSV)

CERTAINLY ONE OF THE most distinctive hallmarks of American Christian higher education, firmly rooted in the experience of the past century and drawing mightily from those roots in this new millennium, is the emphasis that the Christian college or university places upon the integration of faith and learning. It is the topic of endless discussion and deliberation among faculty and senior administrators at institutions of Christian higher education. We tout it among our constituencies. We impress it upon our students. We expect it of our employees. We orient faculty seminars and retreats around it. We look for it in the classroom. We support it through

The Scribe Who Has Been Trained for the Kingdom

co-curricular and extra-curricular programs. We evaluate institutional effectiveness on the basis of it. We defend it before our accrediting bodies. And we write myriad books, articles, and essays describing our experiences with it and trying to pin down precisely what it means.

With apologies for prolonging the discussion and adding yet one more essay to the myriad, I wish to shift the focus of the conversation to a topic that I find largely absent in the material currently available—namely, the nature of faith itself. As a biblical theologian, I shall contend that a clear biblical theology of faith is prerequisite to any other discussion about how we might integrate faith and learning in higher education. As dean of faculty in a Christian liberal arts institution, my primary concern in this discussion is how to equip and encourage faculty members to be the cutting edge faith integration practitioners that we expect them to be. Building on Jesus' passing reference to the "scribe who has been trained for the kingdom of heaven," I shall contend that it is impossible for any instructor to integrate effectively into the learning process something that he or she does not already possess. Conversely, and building upon the same metaphor, it should be impossible for instructors *not* to integrate into the learning process that treasured possession that drives their passion.

The Frustration of Faith and Learning in Christian Higher Education

We generally have a pretty good idea about what constitutes learning in higher education. Regardless of the discipline, regardless of the specific course within the discipline, instructors normally have a clear picture of what they expect students to take away from the experience. This is fairly simple for disciplines that are heavy in math, science, performance, professional studies, etc. Others of us in disciplines like theology, who like to present learning outcomes in terms of 'understanding' and 'appreciation,' are prodded by our accrediting bodies to express those outcomes in more concrete and measurable terms. The result is that we have syllabi and program descriptions across the academic fields that point to specific outcomes of the learning process—what we expect students to take away from our institutions when they have completed a course and when they have received a diploma. So we generally know what we are talking about as regards the nature of 'learning' for ourselves and for our students.

Add faith to the mix, however, and many faculty members find themselves in an ongoing struggle to figure out how to comply with the expectation of their institution. What constitutes effective integration of faith and learning? Is it reduced to a matter of addressing creationism in the science classroom? Does it involve scouring the Bible for passages and proof-texts to underscore the values and principles we teach in our business programs? Does it consist of a simple ritual of opening our class sessions with devotion and prayer? What outcomes do we expect from the integration of faith and learning? Will our students have more faith? Will they be better Christians? Will they have some sort of competence in their field that they otherwise would not have had if faith had not been integrated into the learning process? And how do we know when we have accomplished the feat of integrating faith and learning? Do we rely upon our students to provide accurate feedback on routine course evaluations concerning faith integration? Is there some sort of spiritual development pre-test and post-test that we can apply? How will we defend to our regional accrediting bodies this fundamental identifying mark of our Christian college or university when they conduct their site visit, review our assessment reports, and demand their predictable "Show me the evidence!"? Or could it be that we are asking altogether the wrong questions about the integration of faith and learning in Christian higher education?

As a professor of biblical studies, the greatest challenge I find with students is not so much a matter of integrating faith with learning (as one might expect to be simple and straightforward for this particular discipline), but rather integrating learning with faith. That is, traditional undergraduate students often approach a course in Bible in a dichotomized fashion. This is especially true of students who come from Christian homes and a sustained exposure to Church and faith. By the time they reach college, they have learned and been fed this dichotomy for almost two decades of prioritized status being awarded to public schools over Sunday school. The public schools get five days a week; this is where students *learn* to read and write and to engage with math, science, social studies, history, etc.; this is where students do homework, take exams, earn grades, and lay the foundation for college and career. By contrast, Sunday school and church youth groups get only a couple hours a week and are routinely the home of Veggie Tales and pizza parties. Faith for them has been conditioned to function on the experiential, emotional, moralistic levels and not primarily in the area of learning. Serious study of the Bible is not something to

The Scribe Who Has Been Trained for the Kingdom

which they are accustomed (as they are with algebra, for instance) and so it seems irrelevant to some and irreverent to others to study the Bible in an academic setting. My challenge in this instance is not to deconstruct their faith experience of the past, but rather to help them to do something they have not been challenged to do from their past educational experience: i.e., to integrate learning with their faith, thereby enriching, broadening, and deepening their own faith commitment.

This illustrates, I believe, that we who are serious about integrating faith and learning have a much more important question to address than "How?." Instead, we should be addressing "What?." What *is* faith? What does it look like? Where does it come from? What does it lead to? It would be unfair to say that others who address the topic have not considered these questions. Indeed, everyone comes to the discussion table with some concepts or assumptions about the "What?" of faith. My contention is that we who engage in this discussion have not adequately explored the nature of faith from a biblical theological perspective; and, further, if we do take this perspective into account, the answer to the "How?" question will become clearer (but not necessarily easier to implement!).

This is not a new discussion. In the first half of the 20th century Jewish theologian Martin Buber drew attention to the "What?" question in his relatively brief monograph entitled: *Two Types of Faith*. Buber argued that there is a radical difference between the Jewish understanding of faith, arising from the Hebrew scriptures, and the Christian understanding of faith, arising from the New Testament, and, in particular, from the writings of Paul and John. Buber identified the two types of faith in terms of the respective words in Hebrew (*emunah*) and Greek (*pistis*). The former, he maintains, is understood "from the fact that I trust someone, without being able to offer reasons for my trust in him." The latter (*pistis*), on the other hand, is understood in terms of "I acknowledge a thing to be true."[1] In other words, Buber understands the one type of faith as focused on personal relationship in contrast to the other type as focused on intellectual assent. It is the contrast between how a person relates to another person (I and *Thou*) and how a person relates to a proposition (I and *It*).[2]

If Buber's assessment is correct, then, indeed, we should approach the integration of Christian faith in higher education in terms of the way we often talk about it. For we tend to view and talk about Christian faith in

---

1. Buber, *Two Types of Faith*, 7.
2. See, for example, Buber's companion monograph titled, *I and Thou*.

terms of the "Christian message" or "a Christian worldview"; i.e., faith is a definition of the 'it' of what we believe, rather than an engagement with the 'Thou,' with whom we are in relationship. The problem with this approach is that there are a number of competing Christian messages, depending on what various groups wish to highlight or not, and probably scores of Christian worldviews. Does this mean that there are multiple Christian faiths? Which one, or ones, should we integrate? Are we doomed to the path of sectarianism? Does the slogan "No creed but Christ; no book but the Bible" (as my own church heritage likes to tout!) solve the problem? Of the four approaches to the integration of faith and learning that Arthur Holmes identifies in his seminal work on *The Idea of a Christian College*, the first two approaches acknowledge at least that effective integration goes beyond creedal content to involve attitude and ethic.[3] His final two approaches focusing on [philosophical] foundations and worldview, however, find him in default mode once again to the reigning model of reconciling faith and reason, with a creedal focus, rather than fully exploring the potential of faith as relationship. In an earlier chapter of his book, Holmes recognizes that "Faith is neither a way of knowing nor a source of knowledge. Faith is rather an openness and wholehearted response to God's self-revelation."[4] This characterization of faith approaches more closely the "I-Thou" relationship, but the subtle nuance that this faith response is directed to God's 'self-revelation'[5] and not to God personally indicates that Holmes is not free from the "Two Types of Faith" dichotomy posited by Buber.

Holmes shares company with a host of others across the spectrum of the Christian Church on this matter, however, as is clear from much of the literature on the topic of faith integration in Christian higher education. In a more recent contribution, for example, Stephen Beers and Jane Beers highlight primarily a worldview approach to integration in which "faith is a rational, yet assumed, way of organizing all of the available knowledge."[6]

There is much to say in critique of Martin Buber's "Two Types of Faith," and I have addressed this topic more thoroughly elsewhere.[7] It is

3. Holmes, *The Idea of a Christian College*, 45–60.
4. Ibid., 18.
5. Holmes is referring explicitly to scripture as God's self-revelation, as is clear from the preceding paragraph in his book. Conceivably, he could just as easily refer to Jesus Christ as God's self-revelation, focusing upon the relationship aspect, but he does not do so at this juncture.
6. Beers and Beers, "Integration of Faith and Learning," 55.
7. Lindsay, *Josephus and Faith*, 165–89.

The Scribe Who Has Been Trained for the Kingdom

clear from our literature, however, that Buber's analysis of 'Christian faith' as a creedal assent to a set of beliefs finds substance in the language that Christians frequently use to talk about faith. The German theologian Emil Brunner, a contemporary of Buber's, challenges this dichotomy. Brunner demonstrates convincingly that the New Testament understanding of faith (*pistis*) is, in fact, compatible with the Hebrew concept of faith (*emunah*) in its emphasis upon the believer's *relationship* to God.[8] However, Brunner is quick to underscore that the Christian Church itself bears a good deal of responsibility for giving occasion to Buber's misunderstanding particularly of Pauline and Johannine faith as merely a doctrine to be believed. Brunner identifies four ways in which the Christian tradition itself has misunderstood and misrepresented the New Testament concept of faith (*pistis*) by placing its focus upon historicism, creed, dogma, episcopal institution, and biblicism as the content of faith, things to be believed, which constitute the 'faith of the Church.'[9] Thus for Brunner, Buber's exaggerated thesis confirms the importance of the task of the Christian exegete to take a fresh look at the meaning of 'faith.'[10] As a matter of fact, Buber exaggerates also his portrayal of faith in the Hebrew scriptures with a one-sided interpretation that leaves little room for faith in terms of believing [the content of] a message (as, for example, in Isa 53:1). Nor is he able to remain consistent with his absolute distinction between these two types of faith. Referring to the Israelites' faith in Exod 14:31 he writes: "Where it is said of the people. . .that they believed, that simple trust which one has or holds is meant. . . *When anybody trusts someone, he of course also believes what the other says.*"[11]

---

8. Brunner, "Excursus: Martin Buber's Teaching on the Apostles' Misunderstanding of Faith," in *The Christian Doctrine of the Church, Faith, and the Consummation,* 159–62. In my own critique of Buber's dichotomy, I have demonstrated that the two types of faith that Buber posits do indeed exist in the first century AD, but not in a dichotomy between Old Testament and New Testament. Rather the use of faith terminology (*pistis*) by the first-century Jewish historian Flavius Josephus, writing in Greek, demonstrates more clearly this dichotomy between Hebrew and Greek types of faith. By comparison, I have shown that New Testament use of faith terminology is much more distinguishable from Josephus use and much more in line with the Old Testament understanding. See my conclusion in *Josephus and Faith,* 185–89.

9. Cf. Brunner, *The Christian Doctrine of the Church, Faith and Consummation,* 185–89.

10. Cf. Lindsay, *Josephus and Faith,* 180.

11. Buber, *Two Types of Faith,* 35 (italics mine). Cf. Lindsay, *Josephus and Faith,* 177ff.

A few years ago, I wrote an essay approaching this topic from a slightly different angle, focusing on the need for an inclusive and clearly articulated biblical theology of faith as a foundational requirement for effective missionary encounter with the modern world at the outset of the 21st century.[12] My argument in that essay was that the Church has essentially hamstrung itself by a radical *reductionist* understanding of faith which gravitates to one of two opposite poles. First, there is a pole of 'externalization' which reduces faith to a "non personal set of facts, a dogma, an institutional authority or even, in the case of orthodox Protestantism subsequent to the Reformation, to a sort of bibliolatry."[13] This is Brunner's point, as we have discussed above. At the other extreme lies a radical 'internalization' of faith that displays itself in much of Western Christianity.

In this instance faith becomes an internal, spiritual and highly individualised experience having more to do with emotive response to an inward stimulus than a rational response to outward data. Obviously we may locate in this inward shift a reaction against previous church tradition which placed so much emphasis upon the external. . . .Ironic, however, is the fact that this rather subjective kind of faith is shared by the most unlikely of theological bedfellows . . . [It] is at once the hallmark of the Bultmannian existential tradition as well as the hallmark of a large sector of conservative evangelicalism. For the former tradition a rational belief in many of the traditional, external facts and dogmas is no longer held to be possible so that an internalization is required in order to maintain faith. The latter tradition, on the other hand, while upholding the validity of the traditional, external facts, finds itself hard-pressed to express their relevance for faith apart from the individual, subjective experience.[14]

This polarized and confused approach to faith not only underscores the missiological dilemma that the Western Church currently faces; it also points to the dilemma and confusion that we have in the world of Christian higher education when we want to talk about integrating faith and learning. The models for integration that we have constructed tend to follow the lines of polarization that I have identified here. In commenting about the significant role of student development staff in the integration of faith and learning, Stephen and Jane Beers emphatically maintain: "*The critical ingredient*

---

12. Lindsay, "Towards a Biblical Theology of Faith."
13. Ibid., 148.
14. Ibid., 148–49

is staff members who are intentional about the integration process."[15] While I acknowledge the need for intentionality, I challenge the notion that intentionality about a process is the critical ingredient. The critical ingredient for faith integration is not any integration process; rather the critical ingredient is faith itself. Once we are clear about what constitutes faith, the integration process will inevitably take care of itself.

Faith as "Engaging With God"

Martin Buber is correct in pointing us to the Hebrew word *emunah*, 'faithfulness,' as the primary foundation stone for a biblical theology of faith, even if his own analysis of this Hebrew concept falls short. Our polarized approach to faith, evident in many creeds and Christian definitions, carries a strong dose of exclusivity; i.e., faith is 'this,' and, by definition, not 'that.' This exclusivity shows up most clearly when faith is regarded as the content of what we believe. But it also crops up regularly in other contexts of polarization. The so-called 'faith only' doctrine of salvation is one such example. Drawing on legitimate biblical language and theological underpinnings, many proponents of this particular slogan have misappropriated the language to define faith in narrow, exclusive terms to the effect that faith is something very personal, very internal, as opposed to corporate and external—"a resolution of the will and not a physical act of [faithfulness]."[16] The result is a bland, mechanical approach to salvation and the Christian life where the dynamic, organic interplay between Spirit, word, and sacrament are at best demoted to secondary significance and, at worst, excluded altogether.

Another example of this exclusivity is the so-called "faith of Jesus Christ" debate that continues to engage the pens of New Testament scholars. This particular debate centers around the apostle Paul's use of a specific Greek grammatical construction that indicates a relationship between "faith" and "Jesus Christ" (in Gal 3:16, et al.), whereby faith is the topic of Paul's discussion and Jesus Christ, a noun in the genitive case form, is a qualifier of this faith. The argument is about how to interpret the use of the genitive case form and how 'Jesus Christ' qualifies 'faith.' Is this phrase referring to the faith *of* Jesus Christ—i.e., Jesus' own faith(fullness) which justifies the believer? Or does it refer, as the more traditional interpretation

---

15. Beers and Beers, "Integration of Faith and Learning," 70.
16. Lindsay, "Towards a Biblical Theology of Faith," 154.

maintains, to faith *in* Jesus Christ—i.e., the faith(fullness) of the believer that is directed specifically towards Jesus. It is an interesting debate, to be sure, but unfortunate once again in its polarizing tendency to define faith in terms of 'this' and not 'that,' promoting exclusivity rather than inclusivity.[17]

By way of contrast and correction, the Hebrew noun *emunah* is a much more robust, multi-faceted concept that points us to an inclusive understanding of faith as *both* 'this' *and* 'that.' The noun *emunah* is actually one member of a 'family' of faith terms in the Hebrew language derived from a common verbal stem and expressing different grammatical aspects of the concept. Of primary significance is the verb itself: *aman*. (Even those who have never studied Hebrew, regardless of their own mother tongue, will readily recognize in this verb stem the universal Hebrew loan word 'amen'!) The family of words includes verbal nuances, adjectival nuances, and substantival (noun) forms of which *emunah* is only one. The basic meaning of this family of words has to do with the concepts of firmness, steadfastness, and reliability. From these base concepts, it is easy to see how the concepts of trust, faithfulness, and belief emerge.

But there are other important concepts that emerge from this family of Hebrew words as well. The Septuagint, the Greek translation of the Hebrew scriptures dating back into the third century before Christ, routinely used the Greek word *pistis* (and its own accompanying family of words) to translate the Hebrew *aman* words as faith terminology. This usage of the Greek words was subsequently taken over by the New Testament authors as they sought to give centrality to the concept of faith as the primary way of relating to God. Thus the Septuagint provides evidence of continuity between the Old Testament type of faith and the New Testament type of faith—a point that Buber seemed unwilling to acknowledge or explore.

However, even this one family of Greek words that we routinely translate with words like 'believe,' 'faith(fullness),' 'trust' was incapable of capturing the full sense of the Hebrew word family, so that the translators of the Septuagint had to resort with regularity to the Greek words for 'truth,' 'righteous,' and 'righteousness' to capture the appropriate Hebrew nuances.[18] Artur Weiser, Old Testament scholar writing on the Hebrew background for the Greek *pistis* word group, comments that the Hebrew verb from

---

17. For a more thorough discussion of the 'faith of Jesus Christ' debate and an attempt at a more inclusive approach to this question, see my article: "Works of Law, Hearing of Faith and *Pistis Christou* in Galatians 2:16—3:5."

18. Cf. Lindsay, "Towards a Biblical Theology of Faith," 150.

The Scribe Who Has Been Trained for the Kingdom

the *aman* family has a "tendency to extend into the most comprehensive possible sphere of application, just as [the noun *emunah*] too embraces *the whole attitude of a life lived in faith.*"[19] Similarly, Adolf Schlatter, another contemporary of Martin Buber, identifies a multiplicity of nuances inherent in the noun from the *aman* family that is routinely translated as 'faithfulness' or 'truth.' The sense of 'reliability' that is inherent in this particular noun cannot be properly understood without taking consideration of all of the components together. Schlatter writes:

> That *Good Will* which is closed to hatred and jealousy, that *Truthfulness* which neither conceals anything nor practices deceit, that *Trust* which harbors no suspicion against one's neighbor, that *Steadfastness* which endures by his side through fortune and through misfortune, that *Courage* and that *Skillfulness* which know how to perform service and to offer assistance—not the one or the other of these, *but all of these together constitute [faithfulness/truth].*[20]

All of this points us to an understanding of the biblical concept of faith in very concrete and tangible terms. If we are ever to understand faith as an abstraction of the emotional, intellectual, or even spiritual realm, it is only by extension of the primary concrete, active, and interactive nature of faith that engages body, mind, and soul in consequential relationship to God. But this still sounds very abstract. Can we arrive at a working definition that captures both our imagination and the essence of what the Bible means when faith language is employed?

Part of the challenge is the term 'faith' itself, which has become so ambiguous and colorless in the English language that even in religious and theological circles where a common understanding of the term seems to exist, further definition is still required. But definition, by definition, implies exclusivity—the drawing of boundaries, by which we say that 'this' is what faith is, and not 'that' which lies outside the boundary. An 'inclusive' definition of a concept so multi-faceted as faith requires complexity rather than simplicity. As Hans-Juergen Hermisson and Eduard Lohse have noted: "What faith means for today can only be articulated and understood with the help of the whole Bible."[21] This complexity, however, does not necessarily mean that our definition of faith must be complicated or difficult

---

19. Bultmann and Weiser, "*pisteuo, ktl.,*" 184; italics mine.
20. Schlatter, *Der Glaube im Neuen Testament*, 553 (translation and italics mine).
21. Hermisson and Lohse, *Glauben*, 8 (my translation).

to understand. In the biblical material itself the faith language could be employed—both in the Old Testament and in the New Testament—without definition or further explanation. Neither does 'complex' equate to 'abstract.' On the contrary, a many-faceted concept can be readily understood and appropriated if it expresses a comprehensive and concrete reality or experience.

A comparable and instructive example of what I am talking about with the concept of 'faith' is the concept of 'marriage.' Just to mention the word marriage conjures up for most of us very concrete images. Marriage is anything but a platonic abstraction! But this concrete reality represented by the term 'marriage' is comprised of many complex components—vows and promises, loving acts, sexual intimacy, mutual respect, loyalty, responsibility, mutual submission, shared labor, etc.—any one of which, by itself, does not constitute marriage, but only when taken as a whole. I think it no accident that the apostle Paul (in good company with many an Old Testament prophet) routinely reaches for the marriage metaphor when trying to help his audience grasp the significance of the dynamic, mutual, and multifaceted relationship between the believer and Christ. Can we imagine the concept of faith in this way?

Not far afield from the marriage metaphor, I have developed a personal penchant for talking about faith in terms of 'engagement'—or, more specifically, *engaging with God*. This language of engagement emerges from two key insights I have gleaned (unsurprisingly by now) from German scholarship on the topic. Adolf Schlatter, in the introduction of his volume on the subject, rejects any understanding of faith that is empty, abstract, and irrelevant. He underscores the concrete nature of faith in a term that he coins (but which loses some of its impact in the translation) as 'faith-activity' (*Glaubensbethaetigung*), whereby the concept of faith in its comprehensiveness is able to arrive at its appropriation. In particular, the 'faith-activity' is rooted in the activity of God and cannot be fully appreciated or understood apart from this basis.[22] The flip-side of the coin insight comes from Axel von Dobbeler who, in his work on the concept of faith in Paul's writings, identifies faith as 'participation.' Von Dobbeler, like Schlatter, rejects the notion that there is a general antithesis between faith and works in the theology of Paul and emphasizes the value and significance of human participation in God's own activity. Faith is "the dimension

---

22. Schlatter, *Glaube im Neuen Testament*, xv.

The Scribe Who Has Been Trained for the Kingdom

whereby people willfully and actively participate in the work of God."[23] For von Dobbeler, faith makes participation with God possible because, through faith, personal relationship is established.[24]

The language of 'engagement' or 'engaging with God' captures the essence of this reciprocal relationship whereby God initiates concrete activity and we participate in that divine activity—as the gears that move a car forward are engaged by a clutch. Where, how, when does this happen? That is the bigger story, and it cannot be reduced to a single episode or component. Whether we are talking about the faith of Abraham in Gen 15:3, or the faith of the Israelites in Exod 14:31, or the faith of Abel, Sarah, Moses, Rahab, and a host of other witnesses in Hebrews 11, or the faith of Jesus—"pioneer and perfecter of faith"—in Heb 12:2, the focus of this faith is not primarily *what they believed about God* but more upon *how they engaged with God* throughout their entire lives. When we are told that "Abraham *believed* God and it was credited to him as righteousness," we are not talking about a one-off event or a moment of intellectual persuasion. Rather, the force of the Hebrew term which means "to stand firm" in relationship to another (especially in challenging and trying circumstances where God's saving activity is required), along with the foundational witness of the narrative of Abraham's life, point us to a picture of faith that is characterized by a tenacious and dogged determination to engage one's life with the life of God—the giving of oneself completely to receive, over and over again, and to participate in, over and over again, the saving activity of God in the world. This is the crux of a biblical theology of faith, and this is the foundation for Christian discipleship. And this leads us back to Jesus' parable of the scribe who has been trained for the kingdom.

Who is the Scribe Trained for the Kingdom?

If we expect faith to be integrated into the warp and woof of the academic life of the Christian college or university, the role of faculty is absolutely essential. Effective integration cannot be dictated by governing boards or senior staff. Neither can it be ensured by recruiting the 'right kind of students.' Staff and students have significant roles to play, to be sure, but faculty are key. Let us consider for a moment who is the scribe who has been trained for the kingdom. The scribe that Jesus refers to is a person

23. Dobbeler, *Glaube als Teilhabe*, 4.
24. Ibid., 5.

of letters—a *literate* person; educated in language, literature, and law; in a position to interpret and instruct; quite reasonably a person with 'letters' behind his or her name. The description fits well for faculty members—especially *Christian* faculty members. And, while Jesus is likely referring to scribes who happen to be educated in theology, the precise letters behind the scribe's name are not the main point here. This is not only about the 'scribe' who has a Dr.Theol. or an M.Div., or a D.Min. The letters might just as legitimately be Ph.D., B.A., M.A., D.B.A., M.F.A., Ed.D., M.B.A., J.D., etc. Rather, the main point is that the scribe has been "trained for the kingdom."

The verb that the NRSV translates as 'trained' in this passage is the technical Greek word normally translated as 'discipled'—the scribe who has been *discipled* with respect to the kingdom. Or, in other words, the scribe that Jesus is talking about here is the scribe who is also a *disciple of Christ*.[25] It is one who lives a *disciplined* life of engaging with God—a life of faith and faithful service. Thus it really does not matter what letters are attached to the scribe. She might have a Ph.D. in mathematics or psychology, biology or chemistry; he might have an M.F.A. in creative writing or an M.A. in counseling; he might have a Ph.D. in education or philosophy or history; she might have an M.S. in exercise science or an M.A. in teaching. What is key is that this scribe is a *disciple*. And this is just as important for the scribe who has a Dr.Theol. or an M.Div., or a D.Min., or a Ph.D. in theology; without the *disciple* piece, this theology scribe is not the scribe that Jesus is talking about!

Jesus' parable provides us with a splendid model for the integration of faith and learning. The scribe who is a disciple has an enhanced treasure chest to bring to the table of academia. There is a rich store of 'old things' that the scribe has amassed by virtue of the *discipline* that produced the letters behind her name. But there is an even richer store of treasures available to the scribe by virtue of the *discipline* of actively participating in the work of God. For the master of the house, there is no dichotomy or discrepancy between the old things and the new things. Darryl Tippens nuances this

25. Beers and Beers rightly understand the role of *discipleship* as it relates to integrating faith and learning in the area of student development: "[The Christian student development staff member] must be a disciple of Christ and a conduit for speaking truth into unique and diverse experiences." Likewise they speak of the 'discipleship relationships' between staff and students as staff engage to help students work through routine challenges and developmental issues ("Integration of Faith and Learning," 71f.). I believe the same case could be made—perhaps even more emphatically—for the role of Christian faculty in a Christian university as they *disciple* students inside and outside the classroom.

organic integration when he states that "Christian universities should possess a natural ease in linking one's own intellectual life and work with one's passion for service, love of people, and care of the world."[26] In Jesus' parable, the master of the house unashamedly and without hesitation brings out old things together with the new things because it is *all* treasure. But he cannot bring out what he does not have. Beers and Beers maintain that "one of the biggest challenges for Christian scholars in the process of faith-learning integration is in the determination of how to integrate biblical truth into our disciplines."[27] Holmes laments the fact that "in practice faith and learning interact rather than integrate."[28] Jesus' model of the 'discipled scribe' who does not have to choose between 'old and new' points to a way forward.

If we are serious about the integration of faith and learning in our respective institutions of Christian higher education, we pay a lot of attention to our resident scribes. It is true of the institution where I serve, and common among Christian colleges and universities, that we seek out faculty members who are experts in their respective disciplines, and who are also Christians. We know that a Ph.D. in mathematics does not guarantee that the person who holds the title will be effective in the classroom. We want a mathematician who is passionate about her discipline and who is able to inspire that passion in students—even students who struggle with the discipline. Likewise, nominal Christianity is insufficient to provide the kind of faith and learning integration we desire for our students. We need faculty members who are also 'faith specialists'—men and women who are actively engaging with God in worship, word, and sacrament; men and women who are actively participating in the communal life of the Church and in the redemptive work of God in the world; men and women who, as Martin Luther put it, are 'little Christs' to their neighbors, "giving [themselves] unconditionally to the aid of others," and, in so doing, finding their "true identity as children of God."[29] Genuine integration of faith and learning is always incarnational and it begins with an engaged, or, better, an *engaging* relationship with Christ. Just as it is impossible to integrate that which one does not possess, so also it is impossible not to integrate that which one does possess and about which one is passionate. In this model faith integration is an organic process, not an artificial mechanism. Discipled scribes

---

26. Tippens, "Scholars and Witnesses: The Christian University Difference," 31
27. Ibid., 67.
28. Holmes, *The Idea of a Christian College*, 45.
29. Trueman, "Luther's Theology of the Cross."

who passionately participate in the life and work of God in the world will find it impossible to contain that passion in the college classroom, regardless of the academic discipline. These are the ones who will likewise be able to inspire a faith passion in their students—even, and perhaps *especially*, in students who struggle with faith. This does not obviate the need for ongoing discussion among faculty about effective practices for integrating faith and learning in the classroom. It does mean that we now have a platform for productive discussion and sharing of experiences, whereby we encourage, support, and resource one another for engagement with God in the academic setting.

For the sake of our resident scribes who are charged with this high calling of integrating faith and learning, one final word is in order. It is not enough for Christian colleges and universities simply to expect faculty members to be faith specialists as I have described it here. Faculty members in private Christian colleges and universities are routinely expected to go the extra mile in service to the institution and to its students, and often without additional compensation. Faculty good will and the desire to serve God in the ministry of Christian higher education easily and often result in the over-extension of individual faculty members and the inevitable 'burn-out' that accompanies endless over-extension. Our institutions must be proactive in finding ways and dedicating resources to nurture discipleship and to foster engagement with God among our faculty and also among our staff. I raise the following questions for further reflection and exploration: What kinds of opportunities do we provide on our campuses for faculty to engage with God—at their own levels of Christian maturity—through the ministry of worship, word, and sacrament? Is it reasonable to expect that chapel services geared to the spiritual maturity level of traditional undergraduate students will effectively nurture discipleship in our resident scribes? How do we ensure opportunities for faculty members to share in the communal life of the Church and to participate in the redemptive work of God in the world? Could we envision an institutional budget that prioritizes funding for faculty spiritual development that exceeds the similar line item in the student development budget? What if we were to prioritize resources to send faculty members to engage in higher education—teaching, mentoring, serving—in a mission setting? What effect might that have by way of accomplishing what we want to accomplish in the area of student spiritual development?

The Scribe Who Has Been Trained for the Kingdom

I do not propose to have ready answers to these questions; nor do I suggest that these are the only appropriate questions to ask. A biblical theology of faith points us towards an engagement with God that is multifaceted and inexhaustible. Rather than limiting our focus upon defined doctrine and rigid adherence, we should be exploring ways to encourage and enable our faculty and staff to sound the depths of faith in Jesus Christ. We should leave no stone unturned as we explore and implement what it means for us as Christian educators to participate in the work of God in the world today.

Bibliography

Beers, Stephen T., ed. *The Soul of a Christian University*. Abilene, TX: Abilene Christian University.

Brunner, Emil. *The Christian Doctrine of the Church, Faith, and the Consummation. Dogmatics*. Vol. 3. Translated by David Cairns. Philadelphia: Westminster, 1962.

Buber, Martin. *Two Types of Faith*. Translated by Norman P. Goldhawk. New York: Macmillan, 1951.

———. *I and Thou*. Translated by Walter Kaufmann. New York: Scribner, 1970.

Bultmann, Rudolf, and Artur Weiser. "*Pisteuo ktl.*" In *TDNT*, 6:174–228. Grand Rapids, 1968.

Hermisson, Hans-Jürgen, and Eduard Lohse. *Glauben*. Kohlhammer-Taschenbücher: Biblische Konfrontationen 1005. Stuttgart: Kohlhammer, 1978.

———. *Faith*. Translated by Douglas W. Stott. Biblical Encounters Series. Nashville: Abingdon, 1980.

Holmes, Arthur F. *The Idea of a Christian College*. Rev. ed. Grand Rapids: Eerdmans, 1975.

Lindsay, Dennis R. *Josephus and Faith:* Pistis *and* Pisteuein *as Faith Terminology in the Writings of Flavius Josephus and in the New Testament*. Arbeiten zur Geschichte des antiken Judentums und des Urchristentums 19. Leiden: Brill, 1993.

———. "Towards a Biblical Theology of Faith: Mobilising the Church for Mission." *European Journal of Theology* 6:147–55.

———. "Works of Law, Hearing of Faith and *Pistis Christou* in Galatians 2:16—3:5." *Stone-Campbell Journal* 3 (2000) 79–88.

Schlatter, Adolf. *Der Glaube im Neuen Testament*. Stuttgart: Calwer, 1982.

Trueman, Carl. "Luther's Theology of the Cross." *The Theologian: The Internet Journal for Integrated Theology*. http://www.theologian.org.uk/churchhistory/lutherstheologyofthecross.html.

5

The Transformational Power of Faculty Mentorship

Engaging Newly Enrolled Students toward Academic and Life Success

Angela Long

I REMEMBER THE DAY with vivid recollection as it would become one of many keys to my educational success. It was the fall of 1997 and the leaves had just begun to drop from the cluster of oak trees surrounding the campus lawn. The air was crisp and cold. I clutched my newly printed course schedule and crossed the street toward the entrance of the financial aid building adjacent to the administrative offices on campus. Feeling motivated and slightly apprehensive regarding this new venture, I prayed a silent prayer asking God to pilot my every move and introduce me to the right associations.

I had matriculated that fall quarter as a student in the recently designed Teacher Education program at Northwest Christian College (NCC) and I desired to embrace the manifold learning opportunities that were now before me. I felt a deep calling within my heart to become a professional educator and was cognizant that God had led me to the NCC campus. Only recently, while in high school, I had doubted as to whether or not

The Transformational Power of Faculty Mentorship

college was even for me. I was not what one would call the "ideal" student during my K-12 school years. Yet, God had a greater plan and through encouragement from my parents and open doors to financial assistance, I gained confidence that I was precisely in His perfect will because I had enrolled as a student at this small private Christian college.

Within the first few weeks of enrollment, it became apparent to me that I had found the prescribed environment to tap into my leadership potential. Desirous to meet new people, I had yet to establish any deep relationships. On one particular day, as I opened the double doors to the back entrance of the administration building, I turned into the Office of the Registrar to be greeted by a friendly face from behind the main desk. Unbeknownst to me, the Office of the Registrar was set adjacent to the Office of the Provost. As I greeted the secretary who warmly welcomed me, she began to inform me that the registrar was not available and perhaps I should return another time. It was at that moment that a scholarly gentleman emerged from his office and approached me with a heartfelt greeting and smile. He introduced himself as Dr. Song Nai Rhee, the provost of NCC. Needless-to-say, I was delighted and humbled to meet this man as he proceeded to ask me a series of questions, encouraging me to stop by if ever I needed anything. I was deeply impressed that a man of his authority would take a few moments out of his day to speak blessing over my life and offer verbal support.

Such an encounter became the catalyst for many subsequent meetings over the course of my undergraduate experience and even beyond. Dr. Rhee emerged as a pivotal mentor in my life and encouraged me to take bold steps in education. As a mentor, he emphasized the ideals of hard work, perseverance, servant leadership, and of greatest importance, faith in God. He boldly demonstrated his personal convictions on a daily basis and was an inspiration to my life as he would pray for me, encourage me, actively listen, and offer guidance as needed. Dr. Rhee was authentic in his care and possessed a genuineness of concern that went beyond the typical advisor/student relationship. These many years later, with the support of my parents, firm foundation in Christ, and advising leadership as from Dr. Rhee, I persevered forward to obtain a Doctorate of Education degree. In retrospect, I am grateful to Dr. Rhee for his mentorship role in my life and the high expectations that he believed I was capable of achieving at an early age. His influence set a powerful example to me as a young woman navigating the requisite years of college life in an unfamiliar environment, miles away from home.

Positive faculty-to-student relationships are foundational to preparing students for the real-world and future employment. Engaging students within the first few weeks of enrollment is fundamental to establishing and maintaining successful student outcomes. The focus of this essay is to discuss the role of faculty and administration in taking time up front to invest in the lives of their students through a mentorship model such as that demonstrated by Dr. Rhee. A discourse on the value of mentoring and analyzing the many principles to effective mentoring will be outlined followed by a concluding statement on recommendations to other faculty and administrators in higher education.

Engaging the Masses: The Need for Faculty Mentorship in the Twenty-first Century

Today's college students enter postsecondary education seeking new opportunities and real-world personal connections. As population numbers soar within the United States, more and more young people find themselves "lost" within their own communities as they compete for jobs, status, and a feeling of belonging. With the increase in social media and technology, fewer and fewer individuals take the time to interact at the personal level. Where once individuals felt it necessary to discuss important matters over a cup of coffee in a local café, many now find themselves actively texting, e-mailing, Facebooking, Snap-chatting, and Tweeting their deepest thoughts to a greater world of "friends." While there can be great value in the advances of technology and social media, it appears as though more and more individuals are left feeling disconnected, lost, and alone[1]. The necessity for mentoring at the college level has become especially critical as

1. According to one recent study from the University of Salford (Indvink, "Social Media Fuels Low Self-Esteem, Anxiety (study)") social media may be doing more harm than good when it comes to personal well-being. About half of the survey's 298 participants, all of whom identified themselves as social media users, say that their use of social networks like Facebook and Twitter makes their lives worse. In particular, participants noted that their self-esteem suffers when they compare their own accomplishments to those of their online friends. In addition to confidence issues, two-thirds claim they find it difficult to fully relax or sleep after spending time on social networks. A quarter cited work or relationship difficulties due to online confrontations. And more than half say they feel "worried or uncomfortable" at times they are unable to access their Facebook or email accounts.

The Transformational Power of Faculty Mentorship

students naturally seek out meaningful relationships in an authentic manner and setting.

It is no wonder that select studies have reported that up to as many as 35% of first-time enrolled college students have dropped out within their first year of studies,[2] not to mention up to 50% of all students attending community colleges.[3] In light of these numbers, one must query, "What would prompt a student to willingly withdraw from college having not fulfilled his or her academic goals?" Could it be possible that lack of support, lack of motivation, hindered purpose and feeling disconnected to the campus community are just a few of the many reasons as to why students choose to leave without return? Furthermore, do faculty members have a role in helping students achieve a sense of belonging and find meaning in their educational pursuits?

In a recent 2014 Gallup survey, a group of college graduates were asked if they had a mentor in college who helped inspire and motivate their dreams. Of the more than 30,000 respondents who had earned at least a Bachelor's degree, only 22% agreed that a positive mentor encouraged their life focus and goals.[4] The study concluded that those who had experienced a positive mentoring relationship while in college appeared to exhibit a higher level of well-being and job satisfaction in later employment. Additionally, the study established the many benefits associated with positive faculty mentorship with recommendations to increase mentoring programs and awareness on the matter.

Establishing Positive Faculty to Student Mentoring Relationships

According to Webster's Dictionary, a mentor is one listed as "a wise counselor or teacher; an influential supporter." Effective faculty mentors do just that...provide influential support. Faculty mentors have the power to help mentees to achieve, succeed in school, or prepare for the workforce through a one-on-one relationship that is non-threatening and nonjudgmental to both parties.[5] Personally engaging newly enrolled students (whether freshman level or incoming transfer) within the first few weeks

2. Ccrzadkiewicz, "Why Do Students Drop Out of College?"
3. Long, "Community College Attrition of GED Certificate Holders."
4. Ray and Kafka, "Life in College Matters for Life after College."
5. University of Washington, *Handbook for Faculty Mentors*.

of schooling is foundational to promoting a student's sense of well-being and belonging.

Faculty and college administrators are prime candidates to serve as mentors to the incoming cohorts of students each year. For the majority of these individuals, many have succeeded in life due to the positive influences of one or more persons who mentored them along the way. They are in direct contact with students on a daily/weekly basis and are well-suited to speak into students' lives beyond academe.

Depending upon the level and assessment needs of the college campus, mentoring relationships may be assigned to faculty as a mandatory expectation, or in other cases, carried out more informally by the faculty member as a voluntary act. No matter the parameters by which mentoring is carried forward, true mentorship involves an engaged process where both the student and mentor take time to interact, discuss goals, share experiences, and provide encouragement.

In 2011, I was blessed with the opportunity to author and oversee a mentoring and leadership program called the Pathways to Persistence Scholars program at Santa Fe College in Gainesville, Florida. The program was designed to help at-risk students succeed in their first year and beyond. The core tenets of the program were built upon the concepts of persistence, academic success, servant leadership, and establishing positive support networks. As part of the requirements of the program, students were assigned both a peer mentor and a faculty/campus mentor. During the first week of classes, both faculty and students partook in a mentor orientation luncheon to sign contracts, fill out questionnaires, and arrange weekly meetings. One week in advance, the campus faculty were given a mentoring handbook and prepped to meet their assigned students based upon background, career interests and programs of study. The outcomes of the program were highly successful. Not only did the students in need of support find encouragement, faculty mentors were supported by the college through weekly e-mail notifications, phone calls, and roundtable discussions. The process in its entirety was life changing. Not only for me, but all involved.

The Seven Principles of Effective Faculty Mentorship

The lessons learned in overseeing such a program were transformative. In all, via research analysis of program evaluations, one-on-one verbal interaction, and word of mouth, I uncovered seven principles of effective faculty mentorship. The following are recommendations to help promote positive mentoring interactions among students and faculty/administrators on campus. Faculty should consider the many rewarding benefits associated with mentoring students one-on-one and may do so by analyzing these seven principles of effective mentorship.

Principle #1: Intentionally Advise

The concept of intentional advising is widely discussed but rarely used in many college campuses. The role of advising is perhaps the fundamental marker of what sustains a student in the academic environment. As it has been said, "An excellent advisor does the same for the student's entire curriculum that the excellent teacher does for one course."[6] Traditionally, the process of advising at a college involves a unidirectional flow of information whereby the student is passive and the advisor tells the student the actions to take with a set of checklists, rules, and requirements. Student's take a number, wait for 30 minutes or longer, meet with an unassigned staff member, declare a major, and obtain brief information on the career of their choice. But what does one do with students who decide to enroll and are unsure of their purpose in college? Some will say, "Simply send them to the career resource center to take an online inventory test! The online program answers all categories of questions and will clarify the majority of student questions." Indeed, if that were truly the solution for most students, then why do the vast majority repeatedly fluctuate in their decision making regarding program goals and career aspirations?

Most students lack clear purpose and direction. With no prior knowledge built in of what is needed to pursue specific tracks of study, one 30-minute advising session is not sufficient to adequately assess the needs of the student. Ultimately, the role of the faculty mentor is to utilize a developmental advising model that focuses on the personal growth and surrounding circumstances of the student. Such a model places the student as the active learner and the mentor as the facilitator. In this regard students are asked to seek out answers for themselves and reflect on the reality of their life situation as it relates to college demands. It also requires the faculty member to build a relationship with that particular student and maintain continued support throughout his or her journey. Questions should be addressed such as, "What are your greatest concerns coming to college? What

6. Lowenstein, 2005.

could potentially hinder you from succeeding? What is your one-year, two-year, and six-year plan? Define your college schedule each semester until completion. What will you do should you fail a course? What resources will help you to succeed?" It must be conveyed that whatever the student chooses to do, they ought to have clear direction as to what they want to do and what it will take to get there.

The absolute goal of the mentor is to assist the student through great successes and trials, make frequent phone calls, and establish a working relationship. No matter if the student's journey takes one year or four years to complete, the advising process is meant to help the student strategically map out his or her future goals. In the long run, students are the captains of their own ship. Faculty mentors represent the lighthouses that help direct the ship's movement in the event a storm, land mass, or shallow waterway obstructs the way of success.

Principle #2: Establish Trust through Confidentiality

A student's sense of trust is built upon his or her first impressions. Impressions are fostered through the initial encounters with faculty that set the foundations for engagement. By dictionary definition, to trust is to believe in the reliability, truth, and strength in someone. Long-lasting relationships are built upon trust. With trust comes the knowledge that it is safe to confide your inner thoughts and emotions. In a society where trust is so easily broken and relationships are torn apart, most individuals are weary of trusting. For a student from an at-risk background, trust is a conscious, heart-wrenching decision that develops over time and is not easily given.[7]

In order to establish trust, faculty must be cognizant to interact in an authentic manner, actively listen, maintain confidentiality and provide proactive support to their student mentees. As students begin to reveal in confidence the journey of life—struggles, hardship, fears, hopes, and dreams—the act of full acceptance becomes profound. Faculty, by way of personal example, must be willing to share their own personal struggles in life such as how they overcame particular barriers, learned to persist, and find individual purpose. In so doing, students will discover the authenticity of their mentor and desire to connect at a deeper level. Ultimately, what

---

7. Brown and Skinner, "Brown-Skinner Model for Building Trust with At-Risk Students."

most students long for is personal recognition and validation as having the worth and potential to succeed.

Principle #3: Actively Listen

The act of listening is one of the most fundamental skills needed for effective communication and serves as a foundation to building positive relationships. Unfortunately, most individuals do not take the time to focus their attention on what others are saying, but rather are more concentrated to share their own perspectives. Research suggests that human beings only remember between 25 and 50 percent of what they hear at any given time[8]. To put this in perspective, assuming that one is engaged in a 10-minute conversation with a friend or colleague, the individual being spoken to will remember only half of what he or she is hearing. For this reason alone, information can be skewed and inferences will be made to fill in the gaps of what was not gleaned in the conversation.

Within the mentoring relationship, faculty must become self-aware of their body language and mental focus in order to be fully engaged as active listeners. To engage is to set aside all distractions and remove any barriers that may hinder the communication process. Turning away from computer monitors, refraining from answering phone calls or texts, laying aside work tasks, and facing students straight on are all necessary actions to initiate conversation. In so doing, the environment is laid for meaningful interaction where the student feels "heard" in a nonverbal sense.

Active listening involves the process of not only hearing every word spoken, but striving to *understand* the meaning behind the words. Providing nonverbal cues such as nodding of the head and verbal cues such as "yes. . ., I understand. . ., tell me more. . ., I hear you saying. . ." are all necessary affirmations. Faculty must be cognizant to never interrupt the student while he or she speaks all the while making a conscientious effort to repeat key ideas back. Outstanding mentors who exhibit the above characteristics are able to guide the students thinking toward self-realization and serve as a sounding board of empathy.

---

8. Mind Tools, *Active Listening: Hear What People Are Saying.*

Principle #4: Establish and Maintain Healthy Boundaries

Creating an environment where mentees feel free to interact with their mentors at any given time can be quite comforting to students. However, for the sake of maintaining healthy relationships (and a sound mind), boundaries are to be set and firmly followed. Many mentors make the grave mistake of giving access to their students at all times. This can be done by answering phone calls late into the night and on weekends, "befriending" students on Facebook, and giving out too much personal information. There is an old axiom which states, "Familiarity breeds contempt." While it is important for faculty to practice the concept of maintaining an "open door policy," select students will soon learn to overwork the system. In particular instances, mentees may feel so reliant on their faculty mentors that if anything hits bottom, the first person to be called or visited is the faculty mentor. Indeed, it is imperative that students feel welcome by their mentors and in the event of a major life crisis or emergency, access be given as needed. However, this behavior must not evolve into a common practice as the relationship may become unbalanced.

Healthy mentoring relationships are built upon respect of both parties. Faculty must respect the needs of their students and conversely, student mentees must respect the busy schedules and demands placed upon faculty. Therefore, faculty ought to review the following with their mentees at the beginning of the mentoring relationship:

1. Establish Roles. Create an "Expectation Worksheet" that can be shared and discussed with the student.

Typically faculty mentors discuss their expectations and roles in the relationship such as serving as a guide, friend, acting as a resource person, providing a network of contacts, operating as a sounding board, maintaining confidentiality, and providing support via means of continual follow-up. In turn, students must be given opportunity to discuss their needs and expectations.

2. Confirm Availability.

Agree on the appropriateness of where and when to call. Arrange meeting times and locations being cognizant to refrain from scheduling meetings

The Transformational Power of Faculty Mentorship

off campus grounds unless in a public location such as a coffee shop or restaurant nearby. Discuss hours available outside of scheduled meeting times in the event a crisis or important matter arises. Exchange phone numbers, e-mail, and additional contact information as necessary so that students have the means to contact you. Discuss your preferred ways of interacting. Agree on a procedure to notify one another in the event a meeting must be delayed or cancelled.

3. Clarify Any Limits in the Relationship.

Discuss potential issues that could go wrong in the relationship. Review the idea of "no-fault termination" in the event either the student or faculty mentor desires to end the relationship. The goal of the mentoring relationship is to foster and build-up the student. Though less common, certain relationships are not conducive to either parties and ought to be terminated.

4. Maintain Confidentiality.

Discuss how confidentiality and sensitive issues will be handled. Stress the fact that you are not a counselor and will refer the student when legally necessary. All matters discussed will be kept private and guarded.

5. Exhibit Professionalism.

Maintain professionalism with the student at all times. Inappropriate speech, behavior, and conduct both on and off campus are strictly forbidden. As role models, mentors gain respect by dressing and speaking professionally and maintaining congruence with what is spoken and how he or she realistically behaves in other facets of life.

Principle #5: Act as a Resource Person

An effective mentoring relationship not only involves the act of affirming and supporting, but also places the mentor as a viable resource with regard to academic, life and career guidance. Faculty mentors have a duty to be well-informed on matters that involve the student's chosen career path and academic timeline. Offering tips on the reality of the field and not just the philosophy are critical. Mentors should maintain a list of resources and contacts on the student's select career path and be willing to initiate connections as requested. Exhibiting a level of expertise on various subject matters and conveying this expertise to students is a base requirement. Throughout life we have all relied on others to help introduce us to the right persons, jobs, and resources. Knowledgeable and connected mentors in the field are proficient at doing so and offer a wealth of information on interviewing skills, resume writing, and communicate the social and political structures of the workplace.

Principle #6: Celebrate Success

With each milestone of accomplishment achieved by the student, the faculty mentor ought to take the time to acknowledge and celebrate each level of success no matter how big or small. Ways that this can be done include taking the student for a celebratory lunch or coffee treat, writing a small note of congratulations, calling the student to acknowledge his or her achievements, nominating the student for a college-wide or departmental award, and contacting other program advisors/administrators to share the successes of the student. Small measures of kindness and encouragement lead to fruitful and prosperous outcomes. All too often individuals are not acknowledged for their hard work. Faculty mentors are the perfect leaders to initiate encouragement and celebrate their student's achievements!

Principle #7: Offer Continual and Follow-Up Support

Through extensive amounts of research, speaking with multitudes of students and observing methodologies that serve to retain at-risk student populations, the principle that stands perhaps head and shoulders above the rest may be summed up in two words. . .*continued support*. While it is true that heavy engagement must be emphasized during the first few weeks of a student's enrollment, practitioners must not forget the critical importance of continued support throughout the duration of the student's college career and beyond.

To demonstrate support toward students is to champion their cause, advocate for their success, and provide encouragement in the face of strong opposition. Times will occur when the students will falter and contemplate giving up. During such times, faculty mentors are to be encouraging and positive all the while stressing the notion that true success is built upon the lessons learned from the many failures in life.

As the mentoring relationship evolves over time, faculty must be conscientious to maintain regular contact with their mentees checking in via phone calls, letter, e-mail, or means of social media. It can be easy to assume that all is well with the students when little to no contact is made. On the contrary, it is at times such as these that individual mentees may be in need of the most encouragement.

Ultimately, effective mentors are intentional in their outreach and demonstrate persistent traits to reach out to their students in concrete, compassionate and caring ways.

Concluding Thoughts

The outcome of positive faculty mentorship for a student results in a developed sense of belonging in the college community, higher academic achievement, and increased curricular and co-curricular collaborative interactions with other students, faculty and staff. At one time or another, we have all crossed paths with a positive mentor in our lives that helped to inspire, coach, and cheer us on.

These many years later, since that first, divinely appointed meeting with Dr. Rhee in the fall of 1997, I have kept in regular contact with him and his wife, Sue. Dr. Rhee has been a prime example of one who actively listens, inspires, motivates, validates, maintains confidentiality, and provides consistent and continual support. Such mentoring principles should be the guiding force in actively meeting the needs of all students. As is often iterated by Dr. Rhee, each of us has been placed on this earth for a divine reason so as to make a difference in the lives of others.

In this regard, faculty employees must be reminded of their critical role to encourage and develop their students toward a life of achievement and success. I am a prime example of one who was impacted by great leaders and mentors such as Dr. Rhee, and I hope to leave a shining legacy of outreach to all of my students as was consistently demonstrated to me. In the famous words of Sir Winston Churchill, "We make a living by what we get, but we make a life by what we give." Let this be our mission.

Bibliography

Brown, D. and Skinner, D. "Brown-Skinner Model for Building Trust with At-Risk Students." *National Forum of Applied Educational Research Journal* 20/3 (2007) 1–7. http://files.eric.ed.gov/fulltext/ED495498.pdf.

Indvik, L. "Social Media Fuels Low Self-Esteem, Anxiety (study)." 2012. http://mashable.com/2012/07/08/social-media-anxiety-study/.

Long, A. "Community College Attrition of GED Certificate Holders and Regular High School Graduates: A Comparative Study Using National BPS Data." EdD diss., Oregon State University, 2004.

Lowenstein, M. "If Advising Is Teaching, What Do Advisors Teach?" *NACADA Journal* 25/2 (2005) 65–73. https://www.nacada.ksu.edu/portals/0/Clearinghouse/Advising Issues/documents/25-2-Lowenstein-pp65-73.pdf.

Mind Tools. "Active Listening: Hear What People are Really Saying." 2014. http://www.mindtools.com/CommSkll/ActiveListening.htm.

Ray, J., and S. Kafka. "Life in College Matters for Life After College." May 6, 2014. http://www.gallup.com/poll/168848/life-college-matters-life-college.aspx.

University of Washington. *Handbook for Faculty Mentors*. 2012. https://sharepoint.washington.edu/phys/grad/Forms/phd_MentorHandbookCWD.pdf.

Ccrzadkiewicz. "Why Do Students Drop Out of College?" Edited by Elizabeth Wis-trom. *Bright Hub*, Feb. 8, 2012, http://www.brighthub.com/education/college/articles/82378.aspx.

6

Sixty Years of Change and Challenge in Christian Higher Education

During the Times of Song Nai Rhee

Gerald (Gary) Tiffin

WHEN SONG NAI RHEE enrolled at Northwest Christian College in the winter of 1956, Christian higher education was emerging from the margins of American higher education and moving toward alignment with the mainstream of America colleges and universities. Within just a few years NCC would embrace regional accreditation, form alliances with other Northwest institutions, expand general education offerings, add majors beyond traditional church ministry, and begin to intentionally build endowments. Rhee was part of a growing vanguard of international students coming to America to pursue a college education, many of whom would remain here, as did he. This chapter will overview significant changes, developments, challenges, and opportunities in Christian higher education over the 60 years of his involvement in American higher education, most of the time as a faculty member and then Academic Dean at NCC.

The history of Christian higher education, as with the rest of higher education since the 1950's, has seen an expanding trajectory of exploding numbers of students, new institutions, significant federal involvement and support, and standardization of academic organization and curriculum . . . David McKenna, former president of Seattle Pacific University recently wrote that Christian higher education has moved from " . .an endangered species on the edge of survival . . . to an empowered partner in American higher education with global outreach."[1] In this era many Christian colleges have transitioned from the traditional Bible college model to more complex institutions, usually liberal arts colleges or universities, while maintaining linkage to their traditional constituencies. To that history we turn as a tribute to Dr. Rhee's role, contributions and legacy. Therefore this chapter will include references that give some attention to the history of NCU over the last 60 years in addition to broader trends and developments in Christian higher education.

From the original colonial colleges through those of the Civil War era, most American collegiate education focused on professional and liberal arts education, usually including biblical studies. A direct line can be drawn from Alexander Campbell's Bethany (W. Va.) College founded in 1841 to many Disciples-related colleges and universities today, that also feature Biblical studies in their curriculum. By the Civil War, colleges were expanding curriculum toward applied subjects in agriculture, mechanics, engineering, and other work roles required for a newly industrializing nation. Then came the founding and/or reorganization of universities that emphasized research and professional preparation as well as a wide range of undergraduate majors, often leaving, if not marginalizing ministry preparation to graduate seminaries or theological departments. During this time, the first Bible College as normally defined (Nyack-1882) was established. NCC, founded in 1895 functioned more like a Bible College than a liberal arts college, well into the 1950s when Song Nai Rhee enrolled, preparing most of its students for church ministry roles.

5,454 institutions of higher education operate in the United States today. Not counting proprietary and for profit institutions, about 1600 are private, and of those 900 claim religious affiliation, ranging from a distant affiliation to their historical roots to those deeply tied, funded, and accountable to particular church bodies or traditions. This latter group of Christian institutions form the context for the themes of this chapter.[2]

By the 1920's independent Disciples began founding Bible Colleges to ensure the education of ministers and missionaries at the undergraduate

---

1. Mckenna, *Christ Centered Education*, xvii.
2. *Chronicle of Higher Education*, Summer 2013.

level, eschewing participation in options for graduate study at the time. Other church bodies also founded institutions using this approach to ministerial education (Moody Bible Institute, Nyack Missionary Training Institute) before the turn of the century. Disciples-related colleges such as NCC, Johnson Bible College, and Minnesota Bible College were also established in this format, before World War I. The Accrediting Association of Bible Colleges (AABC), organized in 1947 eventually became the "home" for assuring some level of quality assurance for this undergraduate approach to ministerial education. In 2004 it was renamed The Association for Biblical Higher Education (ABHE). Institutions currently accredited by ABHE are usually single purpose undergraduate institutions educating ministers and church professionals, but unlike early Bible colleges, require a core of general education courses.

ABHE is considered a "professional" accrediting agency, analogous to agencies that accredit programs in nursing and architecture, and is recognized by the federal government to provide that accreditation. Currently, about 200 institutions are listed as members in full standing, applicant status, holding programmatic membership. Programmatic accreditation refers usually to former members who are now regionally accredited, but have chosen to retain a relationship to AHBE for their Biblical and Christian ministry programs. NCC never pursued this specialized professional accreditation but chose to move toward regional accreditation in the 1950's when Song Nai Rhee enrolled. Regional accreditation would facilitate transfer of units to other institutions, provide eligibility for federally based student aid, and increased recognition among peer institutions. It was granted in December, 1962 by the Northwest Accrediting Association, a status that continues to this day. Unlike independent Disciples Bible Colleges, several of whom are now regionally accredited, Disciples and Church of Christ institutions have pursued regional accreditation rather than ABHE, except in some specialized institutions. Some Bible Colleges, holding no recognized accredited status, promote themselves as "accredited" in order to claim that appellation for the sake of student recruiting, church relationships, and potential donors. That is the extent of the benefit, since such status does not qualify students or institutions for the expected benefits of accreditation (transfer, financial aid, etc.), that are now widely considered to be necessary for financial viability.

The first regional accrediting association (New England) was organized in 1882 eventually leading to the formation of five other regional associations, including the last to be formed, the Northwest Association (1923), that accredits NCU (NCC became NCU in 2008) as well as the University of Oregon. These accrediting bodies serve a range of complex research and teaching institutions, but also include smaller liberal arts and more specialized colleges, such as NCU. For many years NCC students were encouraged and/or allowed to enroll for general education courses and elective coursework at the University of Oregon. This greatly diminished when the Northwest Association required the college to provide a full slate of general educations courses for NCC students.

In 1976, an additional organization of Christian higher education institutions was launched by leading Christian colleges and universities establishing what today is called the Council for Christian Colleges and Universities (CCCU). It was founded to upgrade and move member institutions into the mainstream of American higher education in terms of academic quality and intellectual rigor, while maintaining and satisfying their historic church ties. This new organization promised to accelerate recognition of academic parity, assure professional academic disciplinary associations, (ie. American Historical Association, American Psychological Association, etc.,) of the commitment of member institutions to accepted canons of scholarship, and attract the best of Christian students seeking majors not always offered at Bible colleges or more specialized Christian institutions. NCU is a member of CCCU along with Hope International University, Kentucky Christian University, Lipscomb University, William Jessup University and Milligan college, constituting the seven institutions affiliated with the Stone-Campbell tradition that hold full membership among the current 121 CCCU member institutions in the US and Canada, and 26 affiliated in 20 countries.[3] Member institutions must be distinctively Christian in purpose and curriculum, but also provide majors in the liberal arts and sciences, in addition to church related career majors that are offered.

Mission

The founding documents of most Christian institutions such as NCU usually stipulate education for church leadership, pulpit ministry or foreign missionary work, or some other career church role. Since in the past 30 years, many institutions have expanded curriculum, majors, and

3. www.cccu.org/members_and affiliates.

Sixty Years of Change and Challenge in Christian Higher Education

involvement in a broader range of community and professional relationships, mission statements often have been revised, restated, redefined or at least updated to justify these changes. In many cases, the meaning of the word "ministry," has been redefined from referring primarily to education for church careers, to education for "ministry" as in the priesthood of all believers through various professions, careers, and walks of life. This has been lamented by those who seek to maintain the single purpose of a Christian College, but welcomed by those who seek to increase and expand the influence and scope of a Christian institution of higher learning.

The 1928 founding document of Pacific Bible Seminary (now Hope International University) stated that the purpose of the college was to train students for ". . . a fruitful ministry." When non church ministry majors began to be added (Psychology in 1969) beyond those preparing students for direct church roles, the word "ministry" from the founding document was presented as a defensible justification, if not a required mandate, to add majors and curricula as a further means to carry out the mission of Christ. Nevertheless, angst has often accompanied such an expanded interpretation of original mission statements in founding documents. As the interpretation of the word ministry has been expanded, often more students than before that pivot have enrolled in church career ministry majors, still fulfilling the more limited meaning of the word.

Nomenclature

In the last fifteen years the designation "Bible College" has largely been abandoned by colleges employing that nomenclature. This move has been driven partly due to the stereotypes held by academics and sometimes parents that a Bible College is limited in scope, academic rigor, and intellectual stature. In the independent Disciples family of institutions, the 2014 listing in the *Christian Standard* only 4 of 30 institutions, almost all who formerly employed the word Bible in their names before dropping the word, retain the name "Bible" in their official title, with only one holding full membership in ABHE.[4] This shift is significant since among other reasons, it likely signals the attempt of Christian institutions to join the mainstream of respectability and parity in higher education. We shall return to this motive later.

---

4. *Christian Standard*, August 2, 2014.

Not only has the word "Bible" been dropped from the titles of colleges formerly named Bible Colleges, recently there has been a trend to replace the word "college" with "university." Most Disciples and Church of Christ institutions utilized the term "college" for many decades, Pacific Christian College (formerly Pacific Bible Seminary and now Hope International University) was the first independent Disciples institution to change from college to university (1997), now followed by 6 other independent institutions, formerly called colleges as well as NCC. The historic definition of "university" that for decades served as the gateway to this change in nomenclature, has been abandoned in recent years, as some accrediting associations have given up monitoring such changes, allowing for a broader and less traditional definition. Historically, a university was constituted of several colleges (Business, Education, Engineering, Medicine, etc., offering graduate and professional preparation) supported and fed by traditional undergraduate programs. NCU reflects this model today. It is worth noting that when NCC became a university, the word "Christian" was retained in the new nomenclature—somewhat rare when most institutions drop any "parochial" moniker that might signal explicit Christian commitment in favor of more generic and non- religious identifiers.

Since the word "college" refers to high school/secondary education in many nations outside the United States, one motivation for institutions to adopt the nomenclature of university has been to avoid being viewed as a secondary institution (pre-college) by potential international students, not aware that the term "college' normally refers to higher education in the US. Another motive has been linked to the apparent prestige value of the term "university" (Boston College seems to still be doing quite well) to which parents can point with pride when saying, "my son/daughter goes to a "university," offering more status in the view of some parents. Emphasis upon the prestige factor certainly is much more important today than sixty years ago in many sectors of Christian higher education.

This illustrates the sometimes confusing and even contradictory nomenclature associated with higher education. Terms such as junior college, liberal arts, accreditation, university, faith, and even Bible, can be vexing to the uninitiated in the attempt to understand higher education in the United States. Complicating this even more, American universities are tiered into a stratified classification system (masters, liberal arts, doctoral granting, etc) that further differentiates levels of prestige.

Sixty Years of Change and Challenge in Christian Higher Education

Globalization

While it was unusual for Dr. Rhee to travel from Korea to the United States to study in the 1950s, that is no longer the case. 70,627 students from Korea enrolled in American colleges and universities in the 2012–13 academic year, compared to 235,597 from China and 96,754 from India, the top three sending countries of the total of 819,644 students studying in America from other countries,[5] dwarfing the few hundred during the time he arrived. The past sixty years have seen radical changes in world access and relationships through technology, media, travel, common cultural trends and attitudes, leading some to write about a *world society*. Our deeply connected and intertwined world has impacted Christian activity, missions and initiatives around the world, including higher education. Most Christian institutions until WWII were usually explicit about world evangelization as a key component of institutional mission. While that continues in many institutions, it has been muted by new terms, such as "cross cultural" and other less explicit terminology, even when it remains a traditional priority.

The term *globalization* correlates with the current contact, interaction, and assimilation among nations formerly viewed as distant, remote, exotic and often viewed as inferior by the west. Christian colleges now prize and seek international students, intentional alliances, sister college relationships, and partnerships with institutions in other countries, particularly in Asia. Competition for research grants, students, and enrollment of international students illustrate this change. Perry Glazer reports that the International Association for the Promotion of Christian Higher Education lists 595 Christian institutions, all outside the United States and Canada. as evidence of the growth of Christian higher education worldwide.[6] He also notes Christian institutions in Korea now educate 10% of Korean college students.[7] More recently countries such as China and Korea have sought to retain their students by upgrading their own colleges and universities.

The concept of *decentering* is part of the changing vocabulary employed in current analysis of Christian higher education in its global context. If we now live in a post-Christian world in the West, emerging Christian universities in Asia and Africa hold the promise of expanding the impact and influence of Christianity. Non-Western modes of thinking and

---

5. *Chronicle of Higher Education*, Nov. 13, 2013, A6.
6. Glazer, "Dispersing the Light," 324.
7. Ibid., 332.

knowing hold promise to offer new paradigms for Christian impact and visioning. *Decentering* is believed to function to reverse this process, allowing and even encouraging significant non-western influences in Christian higher education. It implies that the Western component of Christian higher education should not remain the axis of Christian education. This can be accomplished through decentering (ready diffusing or even subtracting) the dominance of Western constructs associated with the founding of many institutions around the world.[8] While American Christian higher education continues to lead and define quality and innovation, it is being nudged if not pressed to become more reciprocal in attitude and approach, practicing some cultural humility.

Governance and Finance

Most Christian institutions of higher education were founded by denominations, associations of congregations, local congregations, and sometimes by individuals. By 1950, given the increasing need for resources, the pressure for some standardization of curriculum, the impact of the GI Bill, and the recognition that institutions of higher education function best in alliance and cooperation, the governance of Christian colleges and universities began to change, some would say mature, moving toward its present form. Accreditation required formalized protocols for decision making, employment practices, and fiscal policies. Boards were reconstituted to include not only leading ministers, but also business and education professionals. Board members from the banking, corporate, and management community are now deemed very important given the complexity of financial analysis, fund raising, and locating contacts willing to provide significant support. Presidents have come to be viewed as educators and administrators, not just trusted representatives (denominational officials or ministers) of the sponsoring church. Before the 1960's most professors and presidents (including NCC) were ordained ministers, educated primarily at seminaries or theological graduate schools. The professionalization of administrative, faculty, and governing boards in Christian institutions has led to more efficient functioning while at the same time more closely resembling the rest of American higher education. This raises again the question of what is or should be distinctively Christian about how institutions are organized and function.

8. Johnson et al., "Global Christianity."

Sixty Years of Change and Challenge in Christian Higher Education

As institutions have sought to increase endowments that are now presumed to be necessary to sustain increasing expenses that continue to outstrip tuition revenue, this has engendered an increased risk of a disconnect between traditional constituencies of individuals and congregations traditionally so important for the support of students and financial resources. The waning of denomination loyalty among American Christians, has diminished, sometimes significantly, the number of expected students from sponsoring denominations, raised the expense of recruiting students, and led more and more Christian institutions to govern by the bottom line, sometimes viewed as a pragmatic override of traditional mission and purpose. Driven by scarcity of resources, competition for students, and dependence upon federal aid to students to sustain high levels of tuition, Christian institutions now appear to operate more and more like the mainstream of American higher education, a development that carries both risk and reward. They risk losing their unique role(s) and minimizing if not abandoning their unique niche. But the reward of becoming more relevant for the Christian community and the mission of Christ remains possible, a tension that drives continual assessment, requires humility and holds great promise for increasing effectiveness and contribution on behalf of the Gospel. As it should, this remains a constant tension.

Curriculum

The most obvious change in Christian higher education has been the expansion of majors, broadening of curriculum, with resulting increase in numbers and percentage of faculty outside the areas of ministry and Bible. The inclusion of general education, majors such as business, psychology, education, social work, and other areas leading to non-church careers, has been common for many years in many Disciples and Church of Christ institutions. But Bible Colleges and even NCC for much of its history, even to the year of the arrival of Song Nai Rhee, offered almost exclusively only church related ministry majors. This led NCC to send students to the University of Oregon for general education requirements such as science and mathematics. Certainly the Bible Colleges of the independent Disciples rarely offered majors, let alone extensive coursework beyond Bible and practical ministries or even allied subjects such as English, Communication, or other "practical" courses.

As a whole, across denominations, American Christian higher education, since the mid twentieth century has moved from limited and targeted ministry curriculum to majors and coursework that, on the surface, replicates much that is offered at non-religious institutions. It has been assumed that same titled subjects and majors offered in Christian institutions were equivalent and also justified due to the specialized purpose of the college. The casual observer would not likely discern that.

This expansion into new majors and coursework was been driven by several factors. Many parents now wanted their sons and daughters to study at Christian institutions fearing the impact of increasing secularization (to be addressed later). . .An emphasis on the slogans, "integration of faith and learning" and "all truth is God's truth" resulted in increased comfort with the inclusion of a much wider range of subjects in the liberal arts, sciences, and pre-professional curricula such as counseling, business and social work. Also, the recognition that it takes a critical mass of students to compete in the modern landscape of what it means to be a college, featuring athletics, dormitories, gymnasiums, student centers, etc., has resulted in the drive to expand student numbers, who often seek other majors than ministry and Bible. Finally, the emergence of adult learners in adult degree programs attract students who seek to complete a degree later in life or desire professional graduate education, who are usually attracted by an expanded curriculum. Adult degree programs are sometimes derogatorily viewed as "cash cows" that at best serve to provide funds for the mission related programs on campus. While that has likely occurred, it is not inevitable, and some would contend, has created even more centrifugal drive towards mission. At the very least, in some institutions, more units of biblical studies have been taught in ten years than during decades preceding the introduction of such programs.

It is apparent that Christian institutions that offer a wide array of majors, introduce adult degree completion programs, and offer graduate profession programs in business, education, and counseling often quickly and significantly expand their enrollments and appear to remain stable and sound. This curricular expansion has also led to what some term the "professionalization" of curriculum, i.e., requiring more career preparation courses at the expense of the number of general education required courses. This is somewhat ironic since between 1950 and 1980 Christian institutions were required both by the Accrediting Association of Bible College and Regional accreditation associations to expand, broaden, and require general education offerings. But the more recent trend has been to trim those added requirements to provide more coursework for the "major" or in other words professional preparation, often at the expense of breadth in general education requirements, the key component in the traditional liberal arts concept.

A potential dangerous consequence to the recent trend (since 1980) to add graduate programs, expand majors, and redefine general education—has been the loss of institutional distinctiveness and niche, possibly rendering the former specialized institution indistinguishable from less religious institutions. . No institution can be everything to everyone. Institutions that survive and flourish do so because they serve a particular constituency (niche) and focus upon doing that well.[9]

Secularization

The United States has experienced a series of significant cultural shifts since World War II, including increased population diversity, seismic changes in communications systems and practices, shifts in family systems and demographics, the rise of an obvious drug culture, a sexual and gender revolution, the homogenization of cultures in the industrialized sector of the world and rapid urbanization. The word *secular* is increasingly used to describe these developments and their consequences, even though it does not always carry non-religious implications. For example, in the world of monasteries during the Middle Ages, the *regular* clergy served within the monastery, while the *secular* clergy served among the people in village churches. These factors among others within the family of Christian denominations have formed a substantial part of the framework of challenge and opportunity for Christian institutions addressed in this chapter, creating a continuing agenda for institutions today.

In the last 15 years, heightened concerns related to the above factors linked to secularization have been aimed at Christian colleges and universities. That thesis was poignantly highlighted by James Burtchaell's 1998 report of some well-known Christian universities as having abandoned their mission and unique Christian environments.[10] Other books then followed either echoing this thesis, or countering that his conclusions are overstated,

---

9. Robinette and Tiffin, "Descriptive Characteristics of Disciples-Related Colleges."
10. Burtchaell, *The Dying of the Light*.

if not false.[11] An important counterpoint to Burtchaell, published in 2010 by Robert Schuman that profiled 10 Protestant and three Catholic institutions, concluded that they had substantially remained faithful to their historic mission and sponsoring/supporting constituency.[12]

A component of the concern about secularization has been the issue of openness to ideas that challenge Christian presuppositions and thinking, ranging from social issues to theological convictions. Considering both sides of any issue sometimes carries "dangers" even when considered through the "eyes of faith." A recent research report addresses this component of the secularization issue, based on a survey of 1900 faculty at 95 CCCU institutions in 2007. The study sought to measure the openness of Christian scholars and professors to consider all points of view in research and teaching. The authors of the survey concluded that the consideration all points of view about controversial issues does not equate of increased secularization and inevitable corrosion of faith. Ironically, they also concluded that exaggerated concern about this too often results in "ideological overprotection" leading to defensiveness and rigidity that blunts critical thinking and discourages open conversations and exchange. Some degree of heterogeneity may actually advance Christian faith and commitment more than a strictly homogeneous environment.[13]

This view has been used as an argument/justification for Christian students to enroll in public rather than Christian institutions. Such a view points to the complexity of the term secularization and the possibility that its misuse can work against the popular concerns about it, even as it can be viewed as ignoring the obvious concern of the "slippery slope" implications of the term.

Even though the historic definition of the word secular carries some non-religious connotations, current applications of that word applied to Christian institutions are usually accusatory and derogatory. Reduction of Bible requirements in curricula, moving from required to optional or no chapel for students, employing non-Christian faculty (or even those outside the supporting denomination), increasingly permissive student conduct codes and abandoning required statements of faith by faculty have been cited authors Burtchaell, Benne and Schuman as illustrating increased secularization. While this list usually raises deep concern among supporters

---

11. Cf. Benne, *Quality with Soul*; and Riley, *God on the Quad*.
12. Shuman, *Seeing the Light*.
13. Joeckel and Chesnes, *A Slippery Slope toward Secularization?*

of many Christian institutions, and certainly can be linked to any definition of secularization, they do not constitute an automatic basis for accusing or concluding an institution is becoming secularized. A recent doctoral dissertation by a George Fox University student applied Robert Benne's 10 indicators of secularization in Christian institutions to a California church related university, concluding that those 10 elements, when applied to the history of that institution, did not justify labeling the university as inevitably "on the road" to secularization. Yet, the study raised key concerns and questions about mission and purpose of the university, which goes more directly to the heart of the secularization issue, more so than a checklist of categories of secularization.[14]

A factor often invoked by Christian institutions as protecting against secularization is often termed "the integration of faith and learning." This motto or moniker needs to be carefully defined and stipulated, partly because it is so often cited that some believe it has lost any power to define a Christian distinctive.[15] Badley and Allen contend that multiple definitions and variant uses of this phrase have all but neutered it, similar to the often used term "excellence" employed by institutions to differentiate themselves from other institutions with whom they compete for students. Christian institutions must place Christ, Christian faith, and the biblical text/tradition at the center of presuppositions, practice, and promotional materials. This likely requires at least supplementing and/or expanding the traditional categories of evangelism and world mission to include other Biblical priorities such as justice, spiritual transformation, peace, earth care, and integrity for starters, each of which surely falls within the boundaries of "integration of faith and learning."

Mission and purpose need to be continually revisited, emphasized, and even revisited in order for a Christian institution to guard its soul and unique Christian identity. The danger of overuse of the word secularization is that it limits our understanding of mission and purpose, just as does the word humanism. Each holds potential for helping reconcile our world to God, in the sense that Christian mission surely should be directed to the secular and the human in its various forms and expressions. Therefore changing curriculum, governance, protocols, or revised mission statements often signal renewal of mission rather than abandonment.

---

14. Dummer, "The Simpson Evolution: From Bible Institute to University."
15. Patrick and Badley, *Faith and Learning*, 12.

Conclusion(s)

Dr. Rhee has experienced the most dynamic, expanding, changing, challenging, and risky period in the history of Christian higher education since the late 19th century, when institutions were forced to deal with new economic, psychological, literary, and biological theories that to many, appeared to challenge historic Christian orthodoxy. He became one of a new vanguard of Christian educators to pursue advanced graduate study, then returned to teach and administer in Christian higher education. Early on, he participated in broader scholarly professional meetings, research publishing, editing and earning recognition beyond Christian higher education circles. He was a pacesetter when he began his career as an international scholar teaching and administering in an American Christian institution of higher education. So he is accordingly saluted, valued, and praised for his contributions to the best of our advances in Christian higher education as well as to the heritage of NCU.

Bibliography

Allen, Patrick, and Ken Badley. *Faith and Learning: A Guide for Faculty.* Abilene, TX: Abilene University, 2014.

Badley, Ken, "Clarifying 'Faith-Learning' Integration: Essentially Contested Concept and the Concept-Conception Distinction." *Journal of Education and Christian Belief* 13 (2009) 7–17.

Benne, Robert. *Quality with Soul: How Six Premier Colleges and Universities Kept Faith with Their Religious Traditions.* Grand Rapids: Eerdmans, 2001.

Burtchaell, James. *The Dying of the light: The Disengagement of Colleges and Universities from Their Christian Churches.* Grand Rapids: Eerdmans, 1998.

Council for Christian Colleges & Universities. Members & Affiliates. www.cccu.org/members_and affiliates.

Christian Standard, August 2, 2014.

Chronicle of Higher Education, Summer, 2013.

Chronicle of Higher Education, Nov. 13, 2013.

Glazer, Perry. "Dispersing the Light: The Status of Christian Higher Education around the Globe." *Christian Scholar's Review* 42 (2013) 321–43.

Dummer, Robin. "The Simpson Evolution: From Bible Institute to University." Ed.D. diss., George Fox University, 2012.

Joeckel, Samuel, and Thomas Chesnes. "A Slippery Slope to Secularization? An Empirical Analysis of the Council for Christian Colleges and Universities." *Christian Scholar's Review* 39 (2010) 177–96.

Johnson, Steven, et al. "Global Christianity: Examining the Role of Christian Higher Education in the Changing Landscape: A Review Essay." *Christian Scholar's Review* 42 (2013) 421–33.

Sixty Years of Change and Challenge in Christian Higher Education

McKenna, David L. *Christ-Centered Education: Memory, Meaning, and Momentum for the Twenty First Century.* Eugene, OR: Cascade Books, 2012.

Riley, Naomi Schaefer. *God on the Quad: How Religious Colleges and the Missionary Tradition Are Changing America.* New York: St. Martin's, 2005.

Robinette, Phillip D., and Gerald Tiffin. "Descriptive Characteristics of Disciples-Related Colleges." *Discipliana* (June 1, 1980) 27.

Shuman, Robert. *Seeing the Light: Religious Colleges in Twenty-First Century America.* Baltimore: Johns Hopkins University Press, 2010.

7

The New Creation Motif in the Hebrew Bible

Yung Y. Yang

THE BIBLE BEGINS WITH God creating the heaven and the earth, and it ends with the arrival of a new heaven and a new earth.[1] Throughout the Bible, the term "new creation" occurs only twice in Paul's letters (2 Cor 5:17 and Gal 6:15). Other well-known New Testament (NT hereafter) verses resonating with the new creation idea are: "Then I saw a new heaven and a new earth" and "Behold, I am making all things new" (Rev 21: 1, 5). Given these well-known verses in the NT, one may assume that the term "new creation" is a uniquely NT concept. However, most biblical scholars would readily agree that the origin of the new creation can be traced to the Hebrew Bible, the Old Testament (OT hereafter), especially to the salvation oracles of Israel's three latter prophets—Isaiah, Jeremiah, and Ezekiel.[2] One well-known OT

---

1. The term "heaven and earth" is the typical Hebrew rhetorical expression for a pair of contrasting words or phrases used to express totality, the universe.

2. The notion of new creation is also found in early Jewish apocalyptic literature, dating back to roughly the third century BC through the first century AD and the Dead Sea Scrolls. While it is quite possible that this Jewish literature might have as well influenced Paul's thought on the new creation, the relative importance of this source is definitely after the salvation oracles of the Israel's latter prophets in the Old Testament, their Scripture. Furthermore, possible influences of this source on Paul's conception of new creation are readily available in Hubbard, *New Creation in Paul's Letters and Thought*; and Jackson, *New Creation in Paul's Letters*.

The New Creation Motif in the Hebrew Bible

text is the Isaianic expression of "Behold, I create new heavens and a new earth." (Isa 65:17).

While there is agreement on the general OT influence in Paul's conception of new creation, there is yet a substantial disagreement on the relative importance of Isaaiah, Jeremiah, and Ezekiel in their respective influence on Paul's conception of new creation. Jackson, for instance, argues for the predominant influence of the Isaianic texts on the ground that they contain "the clearest, most explicit Old Testament formulation of the theme of new creation."[3] Consequently, he relies heavily on Isaiah, while giving only a cursory treatment of Jeremiah and Ezekiel, in expounding the OT influence on Paul's thought. Hubbard on the other hand lists all three prophets, yet he definitely pays far more attention to the internal transformation of the individual, a most prominent feature in Jeremiah and Ezekiel. However, it should be noted that salvation oracles from each of these three prophets emphasize different aspects of the promise of salvation through renewal and restoration, as will be discussed. Therefore, a more even-handed approach is needed to hear all voices from these three prophets. In the present paper, we seek to present all voices of these three prophets, while at the same time we attempt to discern and discuss their unique features in the common hope for new creation.

This even-handed approach has an added advantage of avoiding a common error of so-called "prejudicial selectivity" of texts, which has been a common problem in many of studies on the theme of new creation.[4] It is only human nature to favor a certain author and/or text which is more compatible to one's research orientation. But the prejudicial selectivity of texts may predetermine the conclusion. Therefore, we should do everything to avoid it. Assuming that salvation oracles from these three latter major prophets were available to Paul, we can make a reasonably strong case that they would have their legitimate place in influencing Paul's thought in the conception of new creation.

---

3. Jackson, *New Creation in Paul's Letters*, 17.

4. This problem of arbitrary selection of texts to focus on is first raised by Hubbard in his criticism of Ulrich Mell's earlier work for selecting those Jewish literatures which support a cosmological understanding of new creation. Jackson in turn criticizes Hubbard's work for the same error of focusing on those texts which allow him to provide support to the importance of the individual in Paul's soteriology. Interestingly, Jackson chose to focus almost entirely on the Isaianic text in examining the theme of new creation. And so it happens that the Isaianic texts contain both the anthropological and cosmological understandings of the new creation, and also provide support to Jackson's main thesis.

This article explores the origin of new creation, first by discussing how the theme of new creation fits in within the twin theme of creation and redemption in the OT, and then we will explore passages from the salvation oracles of Isaiah, Jeremiah, and Ezekiel in searching for their echoes and allusions in the relevant Pauline texts. Our strategy is to follow an eclectic approach, using whatever methods or approaches were helpful for understanding the particular texts. One can envision Paul who, latching on to the OT theme of the hope for cosmic renewal and restoration, realized in his fertile mind that the promised renewal/restoration of the OT was already realized with the Christ event, especially in the death and resurrection of Christ. This promised renewal/restoration was believed by Paul's contemporary fellow Jews in the Rabbinic Judaism to be fulfilled in the distant future toward the end of the world. As part of the strong defense of the gospel and his ministry in Galatia and Corinth, Paul declared that the prophecies of these three latter prophets of Israel were already fulfilled in Paul's present time, confirmed by the death and resurrection of Christ, which was itself an eschatological event. One may then view this uniquely Pauline term, "new creation," as a crystalized expression for the salvation program prophesied by the three latter prophets and fulfilled in Christ. This notion of eschatological fulfillment for the people of God also has a broad implication to be extended to the renewal/restoration of the whole creation.

New Creation in the Twin Theme of Creation and Redemption in the OT

One may start with the understanding that the soteriological program of the three latter prophets is based on a commonly presupposed view of creation and redemption, which is set forth in the OT.[5] The key element of the doctrine of creation and redemption in the OT may be summed up as declaring and confessing Yahweh as Israel's Creator and Redeemer (Isa 43:1; 44:1–2; 45:11–12). The declaration is, in fact, the expression of their creation faith, which is in turn derived from the worship experience of the covenant community, Israel. While the close relationship between creation and redemption has been expounded by many scholars, it is Bernhard Anderson who states it most succinctly.[6] Citing Isa 43:14–19 and 51:9–10,

---

5. For a classical treatment of the creation and redemption, see Brunner, *The Doctrine of Creation and Redemption*.

6. Beside many classical studies of the creation and redemption in the OT, like

The New Creation Motif in the Hebrew Bible

and Pss 29, 33, and 104 as proof texts, he eloquently declares: "Creation and redemption belong together, as the obverse and reverse of the same theological coin."[7] However, what is at issue is not the existence of the close connection between them, but the nature of that close relationship. Given the vital importance of the twin themes of creation and redemption, what then is the appropriate structure or framework within which one should understand the close connection between them? The answer lies in a special relationship between God and His people (Israel and the Church). The special relationship is perhaps best expressed and defined by the interrelated covenants that exist throughout the history of redemption within the redemptive-historical framework. The covenant relationship as one of the central themes in biblical theology has been discussed by many. But Hafemann's discussion is most helpful for our purpose, partly because of its biblical theological orientation.[8] In biblical theology, God's relationship with His people spans from creation to new creation, beginning with Adam and Eve in the Garden of Eden and continuing throughout Israel's history to the ultimate fulfillment of God's salvation plan. The description of the "covenant at creation" by Hafemann is helpful:

> God's relationship with Adam and Eve . . . provides the basis and contours of the relationship between God and his people throughout the history. There we see that God's provisions of creation for Adam and Eve *in the past* (Gen 1:3–25, 29, 2:8–14) were the foundation upon which they were to obey him *in the present* (Gen 1:26–27; 2:15), and the result of which would be continuing in his covenant blessings *in the future* (Gen 2:16). The interplay between the past, present and future in relationship of his people to God is at the center of biblical theology.[9]

Thinking Christologically, believers also witness the same interplay of times. The Christ event (His death and especially the resurrection), which occurred in the past, provides the foundation upon which believers are commanded to live in the present by faith (meaning that they must trust and obey God's provisions and promises), and not by sight, and continue in

---

Brunner's *Creation and Redemption*, two studies on the relationship in the NT are House, "Creation and Redemption," 3–17; and Bolt, "The Relation between Creation and Redemption in Romans 8:18–27," 34–51.

7. Anderson, *From Creation to New Creation*, 7.
8. Hafemann, "The Covenant Relationship."
9. Ibid., 40. Italicized words are entered here for the contrast and emphasis.

the hope for the ultimate fulfilment of God's promise at His second coming in the future.

While there is a general agreement that the covenant relationship proper really started with the Abrahamic covenant and was repeated in the Sinai covenant, all the key elements of the covenant relationship are also already in the "covenant at creation."[10] This is best expressed in Exod 19:5–6:

> Now therefore, if you will indeed obey my voice and keep my covenant, you shall be my treasured possession among all peoples, for all the earth is mine; and you shall be to me a kingdom of priests and a holy nation. These are the words that you shall speak to the people of Israel.[11]

The beginning words, "now therefore," specifically refer to Yahweh's mighty salvation/redemptive acts in the Exodus event, but the context presupposes that the Redeemer is also the creator of the earth and all good provisions in it ("for all the earth is mine"). They are followed by the Redeemer's demands for faithfulness to covenant relationship ("if you will obey my voice and keep my covenant") and promise of blessings ("you shall be my treasured possession"). The next sentence ("for all the earth is mine") declares God as the Creator, Father and King. God functions as the Creator and the Father through His creation of the "whole earth" and all good provisions in it. And He functions as the King through His intervention or irruption of his created world by judging and delivering his people. Walther Eichrodt states: "that which binds together indivisibly the two realms of the Old and New Testaments— different in externals though they may be—is the irruption of the kingship of God into this world and its establishment here."[12] This divine kingship is revealed through (original) creation and new creation, as well as God's acts of deliverance and protection, judgment and vindication on behalf of his people. The threefold covenant structure of the relationship between God and His people, as represented in Hafemann's already cited work, is succinctly presented below in a schematic flow diagram:

---

10. Dumbrell, "A Foreshadowing of the New Creation"; Dumbrell, *Covenant and Creation*, also has the same notion of covenant at creation.

11. Unless otherwise noted, all Scripture quotations are taken from the English Standard Version of the Bible.

12 Eichrodt, *The Theology of the Old Testament*, 26.

The New Creation Motif in the Hebrew Bible

God's unconditional acts of provisions as Creator/King/Father
—Basis of the covenant relationship given in the past
↓
Commands of the covenant
—Stipulation of Conditions in the present
↓
Consummation of the covenant promises
—Covenant promises or curses to be fulfilled in the future

The text in Exod 19:5–6 and the above discussions make it clear that Israel's redemption is an extension of God's sovereign right as Creator, and the covenant relationship is foundational for the relationship between creation and redemption. One should also note that the threefold covenant structure begins from God's unconditional acts of provision as Creator/Father/King, and these unconditional acts of creation and recreation are the expression of God's *ahavah* love. "*Ahavah* is the dynamic quality of God and God Himself, for God is *ahavah*. The *ahavah* is always dynamic and self-giving by nature."[13] Paul, as an apostle of the new covenant, understands both creation and redemption Christologically. He declares this Christological view on creation in Col 1:16–17,[14] solemnly announcing: "In Him all things in heaven and on earth were created, things visible and invisible . . . all things have been created through Him and for Him. He Himself is before all things, and in Him all things hold together." In Rom 8:19–22, Paul also explains the connection between creation and redemption in the context of biblical eschatology:

> For the creation waits with eager longing for the revealing of the sons of God. For the creation was subjected to futility . . . in hope that that the creation itself will be set free from its bondage to decay and obtain the freedom of the glory of the children of God. For we know that the whole creation has been groaning together in the pains of childbirth until now.

In verse 22, Paul expands the scope of the redemption to "whole creation," and ends with "until now." This phrase "until now" obviously refers the major turning point in the Redemptive-History, namely the death and

---

13. I owe this definition and a nature of God's *'ahavah* love, as well learning to view God's creation and redemption as God's *'ahavah* love to Song Nai Rhee through private correspondence.

14. See also 1 Cor 8:6 and John 1:3

resurrection of Christ. In Israel's faith, time does not move in a circle, but moves toward the culmination of the creator's intention. The accomplishment of that goal, namely the eschatological salvation, finds its succinct expression in one of the two key Pauline texts on the new creation in 2 Cor 5:17: "Therefore, if anyone is in Christ, he is a new creation. The old has passed away; behold, the new has come." Reviewing the relationship between creation and redemption thus far reveals that the relationship may be best understood by explicitly recognizing the intertwining of creation faith within the framework of biblical theology and eschatology. Thinking Christologically within the eschatological soteriology, we can clearly see that in Christ, God's new acts of creation and redemption have already begun. In the same framework, we can also clearly see why Jesus Christ is the beginning of a new humanity and a new history. At the same time, our discussion will also reveal that the scope of new creation is comprehensive enough to cover both the human and nonhuman world, and yet its final fulfillment has to wait until Christ's second coming. Paul evidently understands the new creation in Christ as the eschatological fulfillment of the expectations of Israel's three prominent latter prophets—Isaiah, Jeremiah, and Ezekiel—who maintain a strong link between the redemption of the people and their larger environment. Jackson puts this thought summarily: "Paul's conception of new creation will reveal that this idea (of new creation) is an expression of his eschatologically infused soteriology. It involves the individual, the community and the cosmos, and which is also inaugurated in the death and resurrection of Christ."[15]

How do the twin themes of redemption and creation evolve in the concrete history of Israel? One may start by recognizing that the OT is largely a recounting of historical events. At the same time, "its presentation of history is in the form of a testimony to faith," as Schmidt expresses it.[16] "Faith understands the past," Schmidt states, "as embodying the activity of the one God in dealing with a single people who together are brought in roundabout way into the promised land and who henceforth creates a history that is presented as more unified than it proves to be a searching historical analysis."[17] Grasping the role of faith in understanding God's past activity in Israel's history will help us understand how the creation

---

15. Jackson, *New Creation in Paul's Letters*, 6.
16 Schmidt, *Old Testament Introduction*, 9.
17. Ibid., 13.

The New Creation Motif in the Hebrew Bible

narratives emerge in the context of historical redemption, and this understanding will also allow us to learn about the origin of Israel's creation faith.

A good starting point toward the goal of understanding the origin of Israel's creation faith is Exod Chapter 3, where Yahweh, the God of Israel, presents himself first as the liberating God rather than the creator God ("Then Yahweh said, I have seen the affliction of my people in Egypt . . . and I have come to deliver them . . ."). Yahweh as the deliverer is also found in the Song of Moses in Exod 15:1–21. Based on this observation, Anderson asserts that "it seems, then, that Israel's earliest tradition did not refer to Yahweh as creator in a cosmic sense but concentrated, rather, on Yahweh's 'mighty deeds' of liberation, through which the Holy God became known and formed Israel as a people out of the chaos of historical oblivion and oppression."[18] From this, one can see that the people of Israel confessed their faith from the very start by telling a story, the story of Yahweh's mighty acts of salvation.

In our attempt to better grasp the structure of the Jewish experience, we now turn to the insights of one of the foremost Jewish scholars, Emil Fackenheim, to learn how the creation faith originated in the historical events of Yahweh's mighty acts of deliverance and preserved through Jewish history. In his very short but perceptive volume, Fackenheim shares his understanding of how "this past faith had not come from nowhere but had *itself* originated in historical events."[19] He noted that these historical events were more than epoch-making. In the context of Judaism, he states, "we shall be referring to them as root experiences."[20] He then lists three conditions to so-called "root experiences." First, there has to be a dialectical relation between present and past historical experiences of deliverance. Second, the character of a root experience in Judaism lies in "its public, historic character." Third, past experience has to be accessible to the present. With these three conditions to the Jewish root experience in mind, one can appreciate Deuteronomy's focus on the covenant relationship with God by reminding them of not forgetting "the things that your eyes have seen and the covenant of the Lord" (Deut 4:9–14, 23; 5:1–2). In Deut 4:32–33, Moses *then* turns his attention to Creator God, who created man on earth and the heavens. Along the same line of thought, Hafemann also concludes: "Israel's relationship with God does not start with creation and move forward,

---

18 Anderson, *From Creation to New Creation*, 24.
19. Fackenheim, *God's Presence in History*, 9.
20. Ibid.

but begins with Israel's own experience of God as King and Father at the exodus (Exod 4:21–23; 13:14–16; 15:18), from which she learns that God is also the universal God of the gods and Lord of the lords (Deut 10:17)."[21]

The theme of the creation/liberation of a people is a foundational motif both in the Mosaic tradition and the whole scripture. Along the same line, Gerhard von Rad also argued forcefully that "Israel's faith from the very beginning was primarily concerned with historical redemption and that creation, as an independent doctrine, came into Israelite tradition relatively late through the influence of the wisdom movement."[22] On the same point, Anderson provides another helpful perspective in understanding the origin of the creation narratives in Genesis: "From this faith situation Israel looked back to the primordial beginning, interpreting all history and nature in light of the word of God that had been spoken to Israel. Israel's backward view to the beginning has its counterpart in Israel's forward view to the end when God's purpose will be fulfilled."[23] After explaining the origin of the creation narrative, Anderson moves on to the theme of new creation by stating that "The contrast between God's original intention for the creation and the sorry reality of the present world is so sharp that, according to Israel's prophets, God wills to act, bringing judgment upon the world order so that there may be a new beginning, indeed a new creation."[24] This theme of new creation is most clearly illustrated in the so-called Second Isaiah (Isa chaps. 40–55).

A creative/redemptive work of Yahweh in the new creation is more intelligible when we grasp the OT concepts of the essence of God's characters—*ahavah* (unconditional love), *mishpat* (justice), *tzedaqah* (righteousness), and *hokmah* (holiness). They are concrete manifestations of Yahweh's fundamental nature and also the means by which He seeks to establish His reign in His created world. Of special importance, the Hebrew word *shapat*, the root word for *mishpat*, means making things right, or righting what has gone wrong. In this light, *mishpat*, redemption, recreation, and *ahavah* are inseparably interrelated."[25]

---

21. Hafemann, "The Covenant Relationship," 48.
22. Von Rad, *Old Testament Theology*, 2:53–64.
23. Anderson, *From Creation to New Creation*, 16.
24. Ibid.
25. I owe this insight to Song Nai Rhee of Northwest Christian University in private correspondence as well as to Snaith, *The Distinctive Ideas of the Old Testament*.

The New Creation Motif in the Hebrew Bible

Motif of New Creation in Isaiah, Jeremiah, and Ezekiel:

A common and frequently used method of tracing the possible OT influence on NT text is to identify the occurrence of common and analogous terms and phrases.[26] A direct quotation of the OT text in the NT would also provide another obvious avenue to discern the influence of the OT text. An equally valid and fruitful approach is to identify the common or similar ideas, as well as thought structure, between or among the relevant OT and NT texts, and see how they relate to each other in identifying the possible influences of OT on the NT texts. In a most recent study of the origin of resurrection hope, Chase suggests an illuminating posture in tracing the OT influence: "By looking at certain passages in Genesis, we will be putting our ear to the ground to hear the faint but discernible rumblings of what will arrive later and louder in the words of prophets."[27] This is, indeed, a good advice to heed in carrying out our task.

We will first examine the theme of the new exodus, based on key texts in Deutero-Isa (Isa chaps. 40–50), and then move on to the theme of a new heaven and new earth from the Tritero-Isa (Isa chaps. 60–66, especially 65: 17). After that, we will move on to the theme of the new covenant based on Jer chapter 31, and then we will discuss finally the theme of a new heart and a new spirit from Ezek 36. Our main goal is to draw the parallel between passages of hope for the restoration and renewal of creation in the writings of Isaiah, Jeremiah, and Ezekiel and the new creation motif in Paul's letters. An important point to emphasize at this point is that Paul's term, καινὴ κτίσις, is neither an abstract concept nor the principle of eschatological salvation, but refers to the concrete objective reality of eschatological salvation, which was ushered in by the death and resurrection of Christ. The objective reality of eschatological salvation finds its embodiment in the newly created people of God, expressed as "the Israel of God" (Gal 6:16).

Redemption as New Creation in Isaiah

New creation as the ultimate act of redemption in the face of sins in Isaiah has been studied extensively, and what we attempt to provide here is an

---

26. For a good introductory treatment of several approaches, See Moyise, *Paul and Scripture*, 2010, especially chap. 8 for a succinct discussion of several approaches, 111–25. For the intertextual approach, see Hays, *Echoes of Scripture in the Letters of Paul*.

27 Chase, "The Genesis of Resurrection Hope," 467.

outline of the main contours of this idea.[28] In order to understand how the theme of new creation fits in the overall structure of Isaiah, we may start from the primary storyline of Isaiah. Among several good studies, it is Walter Brueggemann who offers a succinct story line in Isaiah 40–66.[29] The primary message of these chapters, according to Brueggemann, centers around the dramatic depiction of Judah's life in exile and is concerned with three characters: 1) *Babylon* is the oppressor agent who has deported and captured Judah; 2) *Judah* is the helpless victim of Babylon; 3) *Yahweh*, the God of Israel, intervenes as a third party to correct the unequal and exploitative relation between imperial power Babylon and Judah the victim. It is this Yahweh who declares Judah's deliverance from their exile. It is the same Yahweh who intervenes powerfully to do new things. This is the proper context within which to understand Isaiah 40–66.

Within this broad storyline, however, we note that Isaiah contains two strands of teachings in two distinctly different texts on the theme of new creation. One is found in Isa 40–55, focusing on a new exodus, and another in chaps. 65–66 focusing on a new heaven and new earth. What we present here is to rely first on the primary source material and note the parallel and close association of the texts with the New Testament motif of new creation. Several scholars have pointed out that Isa 40–55 contains the highest concentration of creation/redemption language in the entire Bible.[30] While one can discuss and analyze the theme of new creation and redemption in the texts, the evocative nature of declaration in poems can be best appreciated by examining the primary texts themselves. A short sampling of representative texts for the theme of creation, redemption, and preservation are found in Isa 42:5–6, 9; 43:1, 14–15, 18–19; and 48:6:

> **42:5–6** Thus says God, the Lord, who *created* the heavens and stretched them out, who spread out the earth and what come from it, who gives

---

28. Well known and extensive work on the creative redemption is *Creative Redemption in Deutero-Isaiah* by Stuhlmueller. In addition, one may consult earlier work by Anderson (*Creation versus Chaos*, 11–31). For more recent works, see Hubbard, *New Creation in Paul's Letters*, 11–17; and Jackson, *New Creation in Paul's Letters and Thought*, 17–32. I also find that two additional books on Isaiah, among others, are worth mentioning: Conrad, *Reading Isaiah*; and Brueggmann, *Isaiah 40–66*. Finally, Schmidt's *Old Testament Introduction* contains useful discussions on Jeremiah, Ezekiel, and Isaiah, Second Isaiah, and Third Isaiah.

29. Brueggmann, *Isaiah 40–66*, 11.

30. See Stuhlmueller, *Redemptive Creation*, 209–29, for lexical statistics and discussion. See also Anderson, *Creation versus Chaos*, 124–31; and Hubbard, *New Creation in Paul's Letters*, 12.

The New Creation Motif in the Hebrew Bible

health to the people on it. I am the Lord; I have called you in righteousness; I will take you by the hand and keep you; I will give you as a covenant for the people, a light for the nations.

42:9 Behold, *the former things* have come to pass, and *new things* I now declare; before they spring forth I tell you of them.

43:1 But now thus says the Lord, he who created you, O Jacob, he who *formed* you, O Israel; Fear not, for I have *redeemed* you; I have *called* you by name, you are mine.

43:14-15 Thus says the Lord, your redeemer, the Holy One of Israel; For your sake I send to Babylon and bring them all down as fugitives, even the Chaldeans, in the ships, in which they rejoice. I am the Lord, your Holy One, the Creator of Israel, your King.

43:18-19 Remember not *the former things*, nor consider *the things of old*. Behold, I am doing *a new thing*; now it springs forth, do you not perceive it? I will make a way in the wilderness and rivers in the desert.

48:6 You have heard; now see all this; and will you not declare it? From this time forth I announce to you *new things*, hidden things that you have not known.

One of the distinguishing features of the prophetic oracles of Isa 40–55 is that the Lord God, Yahweh, is declared to be the Creator, Redeemer, and Sustainer. This God speaks directly, and declares to forget "the old things," for they have come to pass, and to be expectant of categorically totally different "new things." The use of the couplet "former things/new things" in 42:9 and 43:18–19 is important for our consideration because the same contrast is prominent in Paul's text in 2 Cor 5:17.[31] Isaiah 43:4 identifies the speaker "the Lord, your Redeemer, Holy One of Israel." In verses 43:16–17, the Exod experience is referred to. In verse 18, the speaker exhorts, "Do not remember the former things, nor compare them to the former things. Verse 19 declares the promise, "Behold, I will do a new thing," followed by in the next two verses by "I will," "I give," and "I have formed," clearly showing God as initiator of the promise. In these verses, Yahweh's new acts of deliverance/redemption involve both the restorations of people and nature. Just as the People of God was created by the Exodus from Egypt, Isaiah proclaimed the new creation of the people of God, thus a brand new exis-

---

31. Scholars noted that both Nestle-Aland and UBS refer the reader to Isa 43:18 in their footnote at 2 Cor 5:17.

tence. In this grand restoration, even jackals and ostriches (wild animals) honor God, and restored wilderness and desert (nature) provide support to the people. This vision of grand restoration is the reversal of the curses on the ground (Gen 3:17) as a consequence of sinning against God, and the nature, ever since, longed for the restoration (Rom 8:20–22). The original exodus was spoken of as the creation of God's people, as commonly recognized by scholars, then "the theme of new exodus in Isaiah texts announced a new creation of his people—a new act of deliverance so spectacular as to bring about a complete reorientation of Israel's identity."[32] So we concur with Schmidt's observation: "Thus, for Second Isaiah creation is not really an independent theme that speaks of a primal event 'in the beginning,' but rather it is connected with history and thus with present and future. The creator is the redeemer (44:24)."[33] Schmidt continues: "Like the world as a whole with its light and darkness (45:7), so the coming salvation is a creation of God (41:20; 45:8; 45:8; 44:3a)."[34]

The promise of deliverance of the exiled people of Israel in Isa 40–55 provides the hope. But the scope of redemption expands and is enlarged to the whole creation in Isa 65 and 66. Only two famous Isaiah texts are quoted here:

> **65:17–18** For behold, I *create new heaven and a new earth*, and *the former things* shall not be remembered or come into mind. But be glad and rejoice forever in that which I *create*; for behold, I *create* Jerusalem to be a joy, and her people to be a gladness.

> **66:22** For as *the new heavens* and the *new earth* that I *make* shall remain before me, says the Lord, so shall your offspring and your name remain.

The above two texts in the concluding section of Isaiah are the basis for the cosmic view of new creation. Some scholars understand them to be intended as hyperbolic language or exaggeration.[35] However, it is more reasonable to interpret these texts as the basis of new creation in the cosmological sense, and to agree with Russell that this announcement of the new heaven and new earth "represents in the most comprehensive terms the

---

32. Jackson, *New Creation in Paul's Letters*, 20. See also Anderson, *From Creation to New Creation*, for the origin of creation faith.

33. Schmidt, *Old Testament Introduction*, 264

34. Ibid.

35 Westermann, *Isaiah 40–66*, 408; Reumann, *Creation and New Creation*, 88; Black, "The New Creation in Enoch," 15; and Emmerson, *Isaiah 55–66*, 95.

The New Creation Motif in the Hebrew Bible

work of salvation embracing both the faithful servants and their world."[36] These Isaiah texts powerfully echo the vision of Rev 21:1: "Then I saw a new heaven and a new earth." Continuing to verse 3, one hears again, "Behold, I am making all things new." In this conclusion of Isaiah, God's declaration is an act of deliverance that is radically different and complete in that it is spoken as a new creation in these verses. In summarizing the discussion of the Isaianic texts on the theme of new creation, it is worthwhile to quote Hubbard's comment on the main focus of the two distinct texts: "The Isaianic motif of new creation is both anthropological and cosmological in scope. It includes God's people and God's world."[37]

New Covenant in Jeremiah

In the book of Jeremiah, chaps 30–33 constitute a distinct subsection, often called the "Book of Consolation" or the "Book of Hope." Scholars agree that a range of interpretation is possible for this section of Jeremiah's future hope. While it is generally recognized that a new covenant is the major theme of this section, what matters most in this lengthy book is its basic claims about God, who is the Creator, Sustainer, and who calls Israel to His service. Jeremiah 4:23 reminds us of Gen 1:2 and other verses in Jeremiah (10:12–16; 32:17; and 51:15, 19) all point to God as Creator. This same God will create (*bar'a*) something new (Jer 31:22) or will renew creation. This same Creator will make a new covenant, as in Jer 31:31–34. The most famous text in Jeremiah, relating closely to the theme of new covenant in 2 Cor 3:4–4:6, is found in Jer 31:31–34. In order to feel the full impact and to appreciate the evocative power of the texts, it is best for the text to speak for itself:

> Behold, the days are coming, declares the LORD, when I will make a new covenant with the house of Israel and the house of Judah, not like the covenant that I made with their fathers on the day when I took them by the hand to bring them out of the land of Egypt, my covenant that they broke, though I was their husband, declares the LORD. this is the covenant that I will make with the house of Israel after those days, declares the LORD: I will put my law within them, and I will write it on their hearts. And I will be their God, and they shall be my people. And no longer shall each

---

36 Russell, *The Heavens and a New Earth*, 75.
37. Hubbard, *New Creation in Paul's Letters and Thought*, 17.

one teach his neighbor and each his brother, saying, 'know the LORD,' for they shall all know me, from the least of them to the greatest, declares the LORD. For I will forgive their iniquity, and I will remember their sins no more.

Picking up the covenant theme expounded by Moses in Deut 30:1–10, Jeremiah prophesies that God will make a new covenant with His people. These verses contain several important insights as to the nature of the new covenant. First, this is a *new* covenant, as opposed to the *old* Mosaic covenant. The term "new covenant" appears only once in the quoted Jeremiah text in verse 31 and 2 Cor 3:6. However, the contrasting notion of the old covenant and new covenant is discerned both in the quoted Jeremiah text and 2 Cor 3:4–4:6. As one reads about the glory of the new covenant in 2 Corinthians, the stark contrast between the old and new covenants is forcefully presented—the ministry of death versus. the ministry of life and the ministry of righteousness (2 Cor 3:6, 9). It is interesting to note that the stark contrast between them is brought out for the purpose of the strong apology for Paul's ministry of the new covenant. In spite of all these stark contrasts, however, all covenants of God with His people are the same Covenant of Grace. One can make a strong case for the constancy of God's grace in dealing with His people. (Gen 21:1; 1 Cor 11:25; 2 Cor 3:6; Heb 9:15; 12:24). One may also falsely think that the transformation of hearts is uniquely the NT concept in Paul's epistle. But when one examines even a well-known text for the old covenant in Deut 30:6, for instance, one is sure to find God's promise of circumcising the heart of the people of God "to love the Lord your God" in an unambiguous term.

Second, under the old covenant, the law of God was engraved on tablets of stone and placed in the Most Holy Place in the temple; under the new covenant God will write His law on the hearts of His people. The striking resemblance of this notion of writing God's law, not on tablets of stone but on the heart between the quoted Jeremiah text and 2 Cor 3:3 is another clear indication of the influence of Jeremiah on Paul's thought. With God's law written in their hearts, the People of God now have new desires and capacity to be obedient to His law and commands, and to live a new life in Christ by faith, not by sight. In it the Holy Spirit writes God's law on the hearts of genuine believers (Jer 31:31–34; Heb 8:8–12; 9:13, 14), giving love as moral standards and the power to live triumphantly always (Rom 8:4; 1 Cor 7:19; 2 Cor 2:14). The compelling love of Christ also leads them to the new epistemology (2 Cor 5:16). This transformed epistemology is the

The New Creation Motif in the Hebrew Bible

bedrock foundation for understanding Paul's eschatological perspective, which is also crucial to understanding his notion of the new creation. Believers in Christ in effect become a living temple with His law in their hearts under the new covenant. In this perspective, the new covenant provides the legal framework in which a brand new identity and status of being part of new people of God, or "Israel of God" (Gal 6:16), becomes possible as the direct consequence of the Christ event. As a whole, the importance of inwardness together with empowering people of God in their obedience is highly emphasized in Jeremiah.

Third, as the making of the old covenant (Exod chaps. 19–24) followed the redemption from Egypt (Exod chaps. 12–15), so the making of the new covenant follows the redemption from sins (verse 31:34). In Jeremiah, human sins and the judgment of God (a predominant theme in Jer, chaps. 1–29) is the "plight," as the backdrop, and the new covenant is the "solution" to the grim dilemma.

Motif of New Heart and a New Spirit in Ezek

Ezekiel was a priest (1:3) and prophesied when the Assyrian empire was being replaced by the Babylonian empire under the King Nebuchadnezzar, during the waning years of the Jewish nation between 593 and 573 BC. He was living in Babylon, and the Book of Ezekiel contains as much chronological dating as any other prophetic book. While the two parts of the book contain announcements of judgment on Jerusalem (chaps. 1–24) and foreign nations (chaps. 25–32), the first announcement of restoration of Israel appears unexpectedly in Ezek 11:19–20.

> **Ezek 11:19—20** 19 I will give them one heart, and new spirit I will put within them. I will remove the heart of stone from *their* flesh and give *them* a heart of flesh, 20 that *they* may walk in my statues and keep my rules, and obey *them*. And *they* shall be my people, and I will be *their* God.
>
> **Ezek 36:26–27** 26 and I will give *you* a new heart, and new spirit I will put within *you*. And I will remove the heart of stone from *your* flesh and give *you* a heart of flesh and give *you* a heart of flesh. 27 and I will put my Spirit within *you*, and cause *you* to walk in my statutes and be careful to obey my rules.
>
> **Ezek 37: 12–14** 12 Therefore prophesy, and say to them, Thus says the Lord God (*Yahweh*): Behold, I will open *your* graves and raise

you from your graves, O my people. And I will bring *you* into the land of Israel. 13 And *you* shall know that I am the Lord, when I open *your* graves, and raise you from your graves, O my people. 14 And I will put my Spirit within you, and you shall live, and I will place *you* in your own land. Then *you* shall know that I am the Lord; I have spoken, and I will do it, declares the Lord.

Considering the above two quoted texts with the scathing condemnation in earlier chapters in Ezekiel, we realize that the reality and sinfulness in chaps. 1–24 has to be dealt with before the exiles can receive the promise of a new future in chaps. 33–48. In dealing with the twin themes of judgment and mercy, the fall of Jerusalem (anticipated at the end of Ezek 24 and realized in 33:21–22) seems to be the turning point. The condemnation dominates in earlier chapters (with the exception of Ezekiel's call in chaps. 1–3), while the promise of God to act and transform dominates in chaps. 33–48. However, reviewing both quoted texts from Jeremiah and Ezekiel, it is striking to note the resemblance of putting a new heart in the Ezekiel texts to that of Jeremiah.

In both of the quoted texts above, it is God who takes the initiative and accomplishes through His people what they could not do in the past. The center of attention of God's action is on the human heart and the proposed solution is the inner renewal of hearts in the unknown future. Additionally, we observe a few more interesting features. First, the focus in Ezekiel's texts is on inner renewal in the unknown future, in which God takes the initiative and accomplishes, as exemplified by the repeated "I will" statement. A new heart/spirit in Ezekiel is then contrasted with the new covenant in Jer. Second, we note a subtle change in the tone of promise in addressing Israel as "them" and "their" in the first text to a more direct "you" and "your" in the next two texts. Third and finally, the method of transformation of hearts is by means of the putting "My spirit within you." One should again note the striking resemblance of the enabling Spirit in the quoted Ezekiel text and 2 Cor 3:3, 6. The inner renewal envisioned here is the Spirit-led inner transformation of human hearts. The consequence of such Spirit-led transformation is the willing capacity to obey the God's law and to live accordingly. Yet the realization of this promise is yet in the unknown future. Third and finally, Ezek 37: 12–13, not quoted here, is also quite revealing. As the note for the verses in the *ESV Study Bible* indicates, the vision of national revival is transposed into the metaphor of a cemetery, which may

The New Creation Motif in the Hebrew Bible

be interpreted to the experience of exile (verse 12).[38] At the same time, this verse is also revealing in that while the bodily resurrection is not common in the Old Testament teaching, with the exception of Dan 12:2–3, it clearly indicates such resurrection. The implication of bodily resurrection in 1 Cor 15:12–23, 42–49 is immediately apparent.

Evaluating texts in Isaiah, Jeremiah, and Ezekiel together, we note that the scope of new creation in Isaiah is far more cosmological than anthropological. When the people of Israel lost all the major markings of being a chosen nation (land, temple, and the Davidic throne etc.), as in Second Isaiah, there were only occasional uses of the exodus references, but we find far more use of cosmological references in hymnic participles and in first-person speeches by God (Isa 40:22, 26, 28, 42:5; 45:12). Yet in the writings of Jeremiah and Ezekiel, especially in Jer 31:32–33 and Ezek 11:19–20, 36: 26–27), so much emphasis is placed on the internal transformation under the new covenant. The law 'within' and 'written on the heart' clearly indicate an anthropological focus in their hope.

So far we have sought to explore the new creation motif in the Hebrew Scripture by carrying out two tasks: first by examining where the new creation theme fits in the twin themes of creation and redemption in the Bible, and secondly by examining the parallels between the passages of salvation oracles from the texts in Isaiah, Jeremiah, and Ezekiel and the new creation motif in Paul's letters.

Concluding Remarks

The cumulative evidence suggests several conclusions. First, the term "new creation" in Paul's texts is a crystalized expression for the salvation program prophesied by the three major latter prophets of Israel, which was fulfilled in Paul's time. The fulfillment was ushered in by the death and resurrection of Christ, which is itself an eschatological event. New creation by way of redemption is, in effect, the renewing of creation. One should note, however, that Paul's sense of new creation is not in the sense of the rabbinic use of the term of "new creature" through conversion, but rather *nova* creation, new act of creation. The sense of newness here is so radically new that the only conceivable analogy is in the original creation.

Second, the twin theme of creation and redemption by way of the preservation of the creation in the concrete history of Israel is the theological

---

38. *ESV Study Bible*, 1559.

matrix from which the motif of new creation is to be derived. Within this framework of biblical theology, the covenant relationship governs the legal framework, and it begins from God's unconditional acts of provision as King/Father, which then are the expression of God's *ahavah* love.

Third and finally, the focus and scope of new creation hope in the three latter prophets of Israel is diverse. The scope of new creation hope in Isaiah tends to be more cosmological than anthropological. In contrast, the main emphasis of the new hope texts from Jeremiah and Ezekiel is placed on the internal transformation of the heart under the new covenant. One may say with some justification that Isaiah was keen on presenting the macro perspective of the new creation hope in a series of broad strokes, while both Jeremiah and Ezekiel were concentrating on the micro perspective of the same new creation hope in detailed etching of internal changes 'within' the heart.

Bibliography

Anderson, Bernhard W. *Creation versus Chaos: The Reinterpretation of Mythical Symbolism in the Bible*. Philadelphia: Fortress, 1987.

———. *From Creation to New Creation: Old Testament Perspectives*. Overtures to Biblical Theology. Minneapolis: Fortress, 1995.

Black, Matthew. "The New Creation in Enoch." *Creation, Christ and Culture*, R.W.A. McKinney, Edinburgh: T & T Clark, 1976.

Bolt, John. "The Relation Between Creation and Redemption in Romans 8:18–27." *CTJ* 30 (1995).

Brueggemann, Walter. *Isaiah*. Vol. 2. Westminster Bible Companion. Louisville: Westminster John Knox, 1998.

Brunner, Emil. *Dogmatics*, vol. 2, *The Christian Doctrine of Creation and Redemption*. Philadelphia: Westminster , 1952.

Chase, Mitchell I., "The Genesis of Resurrection Hope: Exploring Its Early Presence and Deeper Roots." *Journal of Evangelical Theological Society* 57 (2014) 467–80.

Conrad, Edgar W. *Reading Isaiah*. Overtures to Biblical Theology. Minneapolis: Fortress, 1991.

Dumbrell, William J. *Covenant and Creation: A Theology of the Old Testament Covenants*. Exeter, UK: Paternoster, 1984.

———. "A Foreshadowing of the New Creation." In *Biblical Theology: Retrospect & Prospect*, edited by Scott J. Hafemann, 53–65. Downers Grove, IL: InterVarsity, 2002.

Eichrodt, Walther. *The Theology of the Old Testament*. 2 vols. Translated by J. A. Baker. Old Testament Library. Philadelphia: Westminster, 1961–67.

ESV Study Bible. Wheaton, IL: Crossway Bibles, 1559.

Emmerson, Grace I. *Isaiah 55–66*. Old Testament Guides. Sheffield: Sheffield Academic, 1996.

The New Creation Motif in the Hebrew Bible

Fackenheim, Emil. *God's Presence in History: Jewish Affirmations and Philosophical Reflections*. New York: Harper & Row, 1970.

Hafemann, Scott J. "The Covenant Relationship." In *Central Themes in Biblical Theology: Mapping Unity in Diversity*, edited by Scott J. Hafemann and Paul R. House, 20–65. Grand Rapids: Baker Academic, 2007.

Hays, Richard B. *Echoes of Scripture in the Letters of Paul*, New Haven: Yale University Press, 1989.

House, H. Wayne. "Creation and Redemption: A Study of Kingdom Interplay." *JETS* 35 (1992) 3–17.

Hubbard, Moyer V. *New Creation in Paul's Letter and Thought*. Society for New Testament Studies Monograph Series 119. Cambridge: Cambridge University, 2005.

Jackson, T. Ryan. *New Creation in Paul's Letters: A Study of the Social and Historical Setting of a Pauline Concept*. Wissenschaftliche Untersuchungen zum Neuen Testament 2/272. Tubingen: Mohr Siebrek, 2010

McKinney, R. W. A. *Isaiah 55–66*. Sheffield: Sheffield Academic, 1996.

Moyise, Steve. *Paul and Scripture: Studying the New Testament Use of the Old Testament*. Grand Rapids: Baker Academic, 2010.

Rad, Gerhard von. *Old Testament Theology*. Vol. 2, *The Theology of Israel's Prophetic Traditions*. Translated by D. M. G. Stalker. 1965. Reprinted, Old Testament Library. Louisville: Westminster John Knox, 2001.

Reumann, John. *Creation and New Creation: The Past, Present, and Future of God's Creative Activity*. Minneapolis: Augsburg, 1973.

Russell, D. M. *The Heavens and a New Earth: Hope for the Creation in Jewish Apocalyptic and the New Testament*. Philadelphia: Visionary, 1996.

Schmidt, Werner H. *Old Testament Introduction*. Translated by Matthew J. O'Connor. Louisville: Westminster John Knox, 2004.

Snaith, Norman H. *The Distinctive Ideas of the Old Testament*. London: Epworth, 1962.

Stuhlmueller, Carroll. *Creative Redemption in Deutero-Isaiah*. Analecta Biblical 43. Rome: Pontifical Biblical Institute Press, 1970.

Westermann, Claus. *Isaiah 40–66: A Commentary*. Translated by David M. G. Stalker. Old Testament Library. Philadelphia: Westminster, 1969.

8

Faith and Learning—Thoughts from a Former Academic Dean

Song Nai Rhee

Introduction

For me the subject of faith and learning is more than a theoretical issue. It is more than an academic concern to be researched, discussed, and written about. It is intensely personal. I am what I am because of it. It has shaped and guided my life of the past 60 years (a full life span according to the traditional Asian reckoning). But for it I would not even be writing this essay.

When I was enrolled at Shin Heung High School in Jeonju City, Korea, in the fall of 1952 as a 16-year old boy I was a typical Korean teenager eager to become educated for good life in the future. I had big dreams. I wanted to serve in the government as my father had done. Like some of my ancestors, I would become a lawyer, a judge, a cabinet minister, and perhaps a prime minister or president of Korea someday.

When I was enrolled at Shin Heung High School, my worldview was Confucian through and through. I had been born and raised in a home with more than 600 years of Confucian tradition. My worldview, my core

Faith and Learning—Thoughts from a Former Academic Dean

ethical and moral values, and the basis of my social relationships were all Confucian.

For centuries Confucianism served as the state ideology of China and Korea. Confucian learning was the standard by which a person's value and social standing were judged, and only those educated in Confucian scholarship were appointed to government positions, from prime minister down to a village clerk.

By nature, Confucianism was exclusivist. One day, a missionary from England met a Chinese young man raised in a Confucian home, very bright but economically poor. The missionary wanted to help him receive a good education and help him become a useful leader for his country, so he said to the young man, "I would like to help you go to England and become a student at Oxford University, the best school in the world. I believe you will become a great leader for China after receiving the Oxford education." The young Confucian confidentially responded, "What else is there to learn outside Confucian classics?"

For teachers and students of Confucian learning, the multi-volume Confucian classics, containing the teachings of Confucius, Mencius, and other ancient Chinese sages, were the source of ultimate truth and wisdom. Nothing outside them was worth learning.

With that mindset I came to Shin Heung High School. Upon arrival I learned that it was a Christian school.

How I ended up in a Christian school as a Confucian is a long story, but I was there because I had no other option in my personal quest for education.

Two years before, on June 25, 1950, Communist North Korea had invaded South Korea. Within a few weeks, my village, all my relatives, my family, and I came under the Communist rule. Overnight, the world we had known came to an end, and suddenly there was a new world, radically different and earthshakingly troubling. The Communist occupiers came down hard on the educated and those who had been public officials in the past. In the course of three months of the Communist occupation, my family and I managed to survive but we became despondent and destitute economically.

Thanks to America's intervention to save South Korea, my family and I became free once again, but we were desperately poor. My family could no longer pay for my high school tuition and books. In desperation, in December, 1951 I joined US troops to help them as well as myself as a translator with little English I had acquired along the way.

While on the frontline, Captain Bill Peterson, a helicopter pilot transporting wounded soldiers for the MASH, and I became close friends. In the fall of 1952, Bill completed his military duty in Korea, and knowing that I desperately wanted to continue my high school education he arranged for me to attend Shin Heung High School, whose principal he happened to know personally. He promised the principal that he would pay for my room, board, tuition, and books until I graduated.

I arrived on the Shin Heung High School campus, filled with excitement. Somehow, it never occurred to me that I would find myself in another world—a world of another culture, and another value system, and another group of people—different from my own Confucian world.

Initially, I reacted negatively. My reaction would have been like that of an American teenager from an evangelical Christian home suddenly finding himself in the middle of a Buddhist school. I was lost and bewildered, and felt like an alien. I was also gripped with fear and apprehension, for I was in a strangers' territory, away from my Confucian world, which had given me a sense of security, comfort, and existential basis.

But I decided to stay and graduate, because, first, I had no other option, and secondly the opportunity for learning there was a grateful gift from my dear friend, Bill Peterson.

Central to the mission of Shin High School was its commitment to Christian faith and Christian values. As an essential part of its educational program, the school imbedded into its curriculum Bible classes and daily chapel services. In the course of three years of study in math, chemistry, physics, history, Korean literature, English, and German, all students were required to study the Bible and participate in daily chapel services.

In addition, the school had a variety of Christian service clubs, through which the students were living out their Christian life. And the teachers, all committed Christians, were striving to serve as role models for students through their caring personal interaction.

As time passed, I began to realize that Christians were not bad and not a group of people to eschew and that there was something noble in Christianity and Christian teachings. Most of all, I learned that Bill Peterson was a Christian himself and had been carrying a cross in his pocket while he was with me in the battlefield.

Shortly before I graduated from Shin Heung High School I accepted Jesus Christ as my Lord and Savior and was baptized. *The Confucian became a Christian.* Integration of faith and learning at Shin Heung High School had impacted me in an earth-shake proportion forever.

My Personal Nurturing at Northwest Christian College (1955–1958)

On December 10, 1955, I arrived on this campus as a new student. I came to this campus to start building a sturdy foundation for my future and my life. I chose a Christian college because I wanted to build the foundation on Christian faith and Christian values.

How did it go? What kind of a foundation did a Christian college help build for me? The following excerpts are from my personal reminiscing at President Joe Womack's presidential inauguration ceremony on October 7, 2010.

"Sturdy and lasting buildings require a firm foundation. So do healthy and stable human lives, and I believed that here on this campus, under the leadership of President Ross Griffeth, I could lay a firm foundation for the building of my life and my future. And such a foundation did this place lay for me, and thanks to that foundation I am standing here today 55 years later.

In the halls of learning and worship here I grew intellectually as my knowledge of history, society, nature, philosophy, literature, languages, Bible and other subjects multiplied. I grew emotionally and relationally as I met new people and made new friends. But most of all, I grew spiritually, in the faith, and on the values that truly matter, which served as mortar and cement holding all other ingredients firmly together.

Here, on this campus, I learned that at the heart of the Christian gospel is the liberating and empowering proclamation that every human being, including myself, is a creature of infinite value and importance, regardless of his or her racial, cultural, social, economic, biological, or biographical background. Here, I also learned about the sisterhood and the brotherhood of humankind, and along with it, my responsibility as my brothers' and my sisters' keeper.

Here, I learned that my ability to make choices is one of the most sacred gifts from my Creator and that we determine our destiny, individual or collective, with the choices and the decisions we make.

Here I learned that doing justice and acting in love are two supreme divine mandates, far more important than vain religious rituals and formalities. Biblically, doing justice, the *mishpat*, I learned, is making things right wherever *SHALOM*, the wholeness and the well-being of human life, is violated, ignored, or neglected. On the one hand, doing justice is looking after orphans and widows, that is, people in need, people without power, and people without voice. On the other hand, doing justice is making corrections where power and wealth are abused or misused.

Biblically, love at its best, the *agape*, I learned, is not selfish but self-giving. While shunning bigotry and falsehood it strives for what is good, what is just, what is fair, and what is true. Such love cannot be hurt or disappointed, because it is also patient, bearing all things, enduring all things, and always hoping for the best in all situations.

Here I learned the existential paradox that to be a master one must be a servant first and to win one must first learn to lose.

At the heart of human life are relationships, for we all live out our lives in the context of relationships of many kinds, and no relationship endures without trust, dependability, and loyalty. And here I learned that these are among the fundamentals of Christian faith and Christian ethics.

Here, I learned that civility in the form of "Do unto others as you want them do unto you" is the golden rule of civilized behavior.

Here, I learned that life at its best is not at the end of the journey but in the journey itself, nor is it in the abundance of things but in the inner spirit able to give thanks, rejoice, and sing in all circumstances including want and adversity.

Here, I also learned that I could gain the whole world but if I lost my soul, all I have gained becomes meaningless.

These and many other gems of life I gained on this campus more than a half century ago through integration of faith and learning in a Christian cultural context. They became the basic ingredients of my life's foundation, like bricks, rocks, steel, mortar and cement for a firm building's foundation. And the foundation has served me well during the last 55 years, especially in troubled times. And in this journey of dreams, hopes, and nurture here at NCU I am not alone. I am only one among a thousand and more NCU alumni who have been nurtured and blessed here."

My Personal Experience as an Academic Dean

When I became the Academic Dean at Northwest Christian College (now University) in 1984, I sought to lift up integration of faith and learning as

Faith and Learning—Thoughts from a Former Academic Dean

the supreme and central concern in NCU educational endeavor. I did so not only because of my personal experience at Shin Heung High School and NCU but also because I firmly believed that integration of faith and learning was fundamental to NCU's mission and its educational goals.

At that time, the subject of faith and learning was also emerging as a major issue among Christian colleges and universities in America. The Council for Christian Colleges and Universities sponsored several workshops and seminars on integration of faith and learning, actively promoting it as the vital part of Christian higher education. I personally participated in the workshops and held several faculty meetings to address the subject and to cooperatively explore ways to practice it on NCU campus.

During my tenure as the Academic Dean, however, I remained frustrated as discussions of the subject continued among Christian college administrators and faculty nationally as well as locally. The biggest problem was the ambiguity surrounding the phrase, integration of faith and learning. What is meant by faith? What is meant by learning? And what is meant by integration? By faith do we mean a set of doctrines or faith statements? By learning, do we mean knowledge in history, literature, math, biology, geology, chemistry, music, etc.? By integration do we mean reconciling each and every piece of information, say in math, history, philosophy, or chemistry, with the Christian faith, and if so with what aspect of the faith?

This latter question became the most vexing issue for all concerned as it became apparent that few or no instructor in humanities, social sciences, and sciences was adequately prepared theologically or biblically to relate their fields to faith. By the same token few or no biblical and theological instructor was sufficiently prepared academically to relate faith to the said various academic disciplines.

Along the way, I painfully realized that integration of faith and learning was much easier said than done. The faculty and I agreed that it was a critically important and essential concern and a supreme goal of NCU education, but we were all lost on "what it meant" and "how to do it."

In looking back today I realize that we all missed the point. We were asking the wrong questions, and our focus was misdirected.

My Current Perceptions on Faith and Learning

Even after I retired from the deanship, I have continued to ponder on the subject. And after more than 30 years of thinking, I have reached the following conclusions:

First, *integration of Christian faith and learning is the heart, the soul, and the substance of intentionally Christian higher education.*

It is the primary means by which NCU, which proudly claims to be a Christ-centered community, fulfills its institutional mission and educational goals and objectives, including life-transformation in Christ and discovering God's call in life, work, and service.

Second, *integration of faith and learning is the primary modus operandi by which a Christian culture is created, nurtured, and sustained on the campuses of intentionally Christian colleges and universities.*

Culture is learned or cultivated behavior or the totality of knowledge, experience, and behavior which a person gains in a particular cultural and social context.

As such, culture is also the *context* in which humans learn to communicate, think, behave, and survive as humans. American culture is the primary context in which a child born in America learns to talk, think, behave, and survive as an American. If the same child were born in another cultural context, say Chinese culture, that child learns to talk, think, behave, and survive as a Chinese.

Likewise it is only within the Christian cultural context that a student learns to talk, think, behave, and live as a Christian. In Christian colleges and universities, the Christian culture is created, nurtured, and sustained through integration of faith and learning.

Third, *integration of faith and learning is NOT reconciliation of knowledge and faith*. It is not an exercise of Christian apologetic. That is, it is not an effort to reconcile math, history, or chemistry with the Christian faith or vice versa. Such efforts are impractical and impossible.

Rather, integration of faith and learning is an effort to bring Christian meaning into all knowledge in light of the transcendent Christian faith and worldview. It is a conscious effort to help students become informed of the message of the Christian gospel and the fundamental Christian values and become impacted by them in their life and work. It is a means by which a Christian culture is created, nurtured, and sustained on a Christian college campus.

Faith and Learning—Thoughts from a Former Academic Dean

Fourthly, *integration of Christian faith and learning is practical. It can be achieved through a four-pronged approach.*

1. Embed a Bible class and a class on Christian values into the general requirements.

    The Bible class should be designed to lift up major themes—especially, creation, fall, and redemption—and inspiring Biblical personalities so as to inspire students to live a life reflecting Christian faith and values.

    In this effort, when I was teaching the Old Testament I created a freshman OT class called "Great Themes and Personalities in the Old Testament." I thought the class was quite effective. NCU could create two required freshmen classes entitled "Great Themes and Personalities in the Bible I: the Old Testament" and "Great Themes and Personalities in the Bible II: the New Testament."

    (I found that the traditional "general introduction of the Old and the New Testament" courses were of little value in integration of faith and learning.)

    The class on Christian values would focus on those ethical and moral values which are universally regarded as Christian regardless of church or personal stances: justice, peace, reconciliation, sanctity of life, covenant and covenant community, empathetic love, active compassion, service or servant-hood, the Golden Rule, the Sermon on the Mount, Paul's teaching on *agape* love (1 Corinthians 13 among others).

    Controversial issues may also be discussed, with differing views and their reasons presented, in carefully and sensitively designed formats. (NCU has done these, but it needs to review the current offerings.)

2. Make chapel/worship an integral component of the general requirements.

    In the chapel students hear inspiring messages about Christian faith, life, and service. In addition to chapel, regular devotions should be encouraged at dormitory and other student housing venues. These enhance students' awareness of the importance of worship and prayer essential to Christian faith and life. (NCU has already been doing this.)

3. NCU should proactively sponsor one or two special lectureships per year focusing on a specific academic area.

    There are Christian scholars/professors who have done a lot of thinking and publishing on integration of faith and learning in a specific academic subject area. They should be invited to the campus for a special lectureship and interaction with students in classes.

4. Everyone in the faculty and the staff should intentionally strive to be a role model in living and practicing the Christian faith in their personal relationship with students.

In this regard, developing a close, warm, trusting relationship with students has always been very helpful. Wherever and whenever possible and/or appropriate, faculty members should share their Christian faith with students.

Finally, to make the four-pronged approach to integration of faith and learning work on a regular and ongoing basis, the whole NCU community must be proactive.

To that end, there should be a standing committee on integration of faith and learning, chaired by the academic dean and consisting of the president, academic dean, and heads of all academic divisions and a representative of the staff. The committee would meet regularly to review the progress, the needs, and the issues in integrating faith and learning in NCU education in light of the four-pronged approach and make positive and constructive adjustments along the way.

Conclusion

In many ways, the world of today is less kind, less secure, and less assuring than 55 years ago. Things are changing too fast. Values and perspectives are changing often in ways defying even our simple common sense. Greed is considered good, irresponsibility is rewarded, and self-interest reigns as the all-dominant motivational force. Violence has become the normative theme in the entertainment industry as well as in many real life settings. Our children can no longer walk to school by themselves. As for civility, it has become the thing of the past. Lives and relationships of individuals, institutions, and corporations, built on sand, are falling apart or have crumbled before our very eyes. And we wonder and ask: What's happening? Will chaos carry the day? What's the right thing to do? Where can I find the anchor that will hold me down secure in the midst of swirling waters? Where can I find a solid ground to stand on? Where do I go to find the basic ingredients I need for a firm and secure foundation for my life, for my children and my grandchildren, and for my society?

Faith and Learning—Thoughts from a Former Academic Dean

Here in the eastern part of Eugene, we have two great institutions of higher learning: University of Oregon and Northwest Christian University, standing side by side. The two have much in common but the two are also distinctly different in their missions. The commonality and the distinction are well illustrated by the words permanently inscribed on the front walls of their libraries. On the wall above the main entrances of the University of Oregon Library are found the immortal words of Jesus: "You will know the truth and the truth will make you free." This quotation from the New Testament (John 8:32) appears along with words, nature, philosophy, art, literature, history, and government," the various subjects for which the Knight Library holds tens of thousands of books. Through these permanently inscribed words, the University seeks to articulate its mission, namely, helping its students, among other purposes, become free from ignorance about nature, history, and the world and lead an enlightened life with the help of the library resources and instruction in various academic disciplines.

On the wall next to the original main entrance of NCU Library are also permanently inscribed words, which articulate ITS mission: "Books and the Book. That we may know Him." Books and the Book that we may know Him, that is, the one who spoke the immortal words, "You will know the truth and the truth will make you free."

Here, at Northwest Christian University, we also expect that the students be freed from ignorance about nature, history, and the world through the study of science, history, philosophy and other academic disciplines and lead an enlightened life, as at the University and other academic institutions. But, here we expect them to go beyond freedom from ignorance and KNOW the ONE who spoke the immortal words, "You will know the truth, and the truth will make you free," because we firmly believe that the ultimate meaning of our life lies beyond ignorance and freedom and that it resides in existentially and transformationally relating to Jesus Christ, who himself IS the truth, the way, and the life.

For this reason, the joining of the chapel and the library physically and architecturally in 1995, under the leadership of President James Womack, was one of the most meaningful events in the history of this University. Physically and symbolically, the event was proclaiming loudly to the world and to everyone on this campus that integration of faith and learning is the primary mission of this place, on the belief that faith in Christ acts as mortar and cement firmly holding all essential ingredients together for genuine and lasting life as with cement holding bricks, rocks, and steel for firm foundations of lasting structures.

As envisioned by its founders, James Bushnell and Eugene Sanderson, and undergirded for more than a century by other leaders and benefactors, Kendal Burke, Ross Griffeth, Victor Hoven, William Richardson, Ansel Hyland, James Stock, Lottie Price, and countless other friends, that sacred mission remains unchanged.

Integration of faith and learning is the heart, the soul, and the substance of Christian colleges and universities. Its primary goal is to help create a Christian culture and not to engage in Christian apologetic. It is practical with the four-pronged approach described above. The administration, the faculty, and the staff must pursue it proactively and intentionally, through a standing committee, to make it a vital part of every Christian learning community.

www.ingramcontent.com/pod-product-compliance
Lightning Source LLC
Chambersburg PA
CBHW051942160426
43198CB00013B/2264